Themes for Today

A Beginning
Reading Skills Text

Lorraine C. Smith
Nancy Nici Mare

English Language Institute
Queens College
The City University of New York

Illustrations by
Joseph Tenga

Heinle & Heinle Publishers
A Division of International Thomson Publishing, Inc.
Boston, Massachusetts 02116 U.S.A.

Pacific Grove • Albany • Boston • Cincinnati • Detroit • London • Madrid • Melbourne
Mexico City • New York • Paris • San Francisco • Tokyo • Toronto • Washington

The publication of *Themes for Today: A Beginning Reading Skills Text* was directed by the members of the Newbury House Publishing Team at Heinle & Heinle:

Erik Gundersen, Editorial Director
John F. McHugh, Market Development Director
Kristin Thalheimer, Production Services Coordinator

Also participating in the publication of this program were:
Publisher: Stanley J. Galek
Director of Production: Elizabeth Holthaus
Project Manager: LeGwin Associates
Senior Assistant Editor: Ken Pratt
Manufacturing Coordinator: Mary Beth Hennebury
Photo/Video Specialist: Jonathan Stark
Cover Design: Kim Wedlake

Credits as indicated for photographs listed below:
p. 1, Ira Kirschenbaum/Stock•Boston; p. 2, Chuck Davis/Tony Stone Images; p. 80, Owen Franken/Stock•Boston; p. 95 Homer Sykes/Woodfin Camp and Associates; p. 96, AP/World Wide Photos; p. 101, UPI/Bettman; pps. 110 and 127, The Bettman Archive; p. 163, Reuters/Bettman; p. 164, Photo by National Severe Storms Laboratory, National Oceanic and Atmospheric Administration; p. 170, UPI/Bettman Newsphotos.

All other photographs and illustrations are by Joseph Tenga. The photo on p. 16 by Joseph Tenga, courtesy of the Brooklyn Museum; on p. 146 by Joseph Tenga, from: Santarem Atlas, in the Map Division, New York Public Library, Astor, Lenox and Tilden Foundation; and on p. 155 by Joseph Tenga, from: Nova Totious Terrarum, in the Map Division, New York Public Library, Astor, Lenonx and Tilden Foundation.

Heinle & Heinle Publishers is a division of International Thomson Publishing, Inc.

Manufactured in the United States of America

Library of Congress Cataloging in Publication Data

Library of Congress Cataloging-in-Publication Data
Smith, Lorraine C.
    Themes for today : a beginning reading skills text / Lorraine C. Smith, Nancy Nici Mare : illustrations by Joseph Tenga.
         p. cm.
    Includes index.
    ISBN 0-8384-5252-3
    1. English language—Textbooks for foreign speakers. 2. Readers.
I. Mare, Nancy Nici, 1957–   . II. Title.
PE1128.S5849   1995
428.6'4—dc20   95–45909
                                                              CIP

ISBN: 0-8384-5252-3

1 2 3 4 5 6 7 8 9 10 XXX 01 00 99 97 96 95

for Tom

Contents

Preface

Themes for Today is a reading skills text intended for academically oriented students of English as a second or foreign language who have had at least some exposure to English. *Themes for Today* encompasses such areas as health, history, science, and technology. Experience has shown that college-bound students are interested in working with more academic subjects than are often found in ESL texts at the lower level. At the same time, beginning ESL students need to work with topics that they have some familiarity with—those topics for which they have some background knowledge to draw on.

Themes for Today is one in a series of reading skills texts. The complete series has been designed to meet the needs of students from the beginning to the advanced levels and includes the following:

- *Themes for Today.* .... beginning
- *Insights for Today* .... high beginning
- *Issues for Today* .... intermediate
- *Concepts for Today* .... high intermediate
- *Topics for Today* .... advanced

Themes for Today provides students with essential practice in the type of reading skills they will need in an academic environment. It requires students to not only read text, but also to extract basic information from charts, graphs, illustrations, and photographs. Beginning level students are rarely exposed to this type of reading material. Furthermore, the students are given the opportunity to speak and write about their own experiences, country, and culture in English, and to compare them with those of the United States and other countries. This text has real-life activities that give students specific tasks to complete. Furthermore, all four skills —reading, writing, speaking, and listening—are incorporated into each chapter.

This text consists of six units. Each unit contains two chapters that deal with related subjects. At the same time, though, each chapter is entirely separate in content from the other chapter contained in that unit. This format gives the instructor the option of either completing entire units or choosing individual chapters as a focus.

The opening illustrations and the initial exercise preceding each reading encourage the students to think about the ideas, facts, and vocabulary that will be presented in the passage. Discussing illustrations in class helps lower level students visualize what they are going to read about and gives them cues for the new vocabulary they will encounter. Working in groups to activate and discuss prior knowledge of a subject helps enhance reading comprehension.

Readers, especially beginning second language readers, vary considerably in their strategy use and comprehension monitoring activities. Some readers benefit more from focusing on reading one or two paragraphs at a time and checking their comprehension before continuing to read. Other readers may prefer to read an entire passage and then consider questions related to the reading. Consequently, in order to provide maximum flexibility, all the reading passages are presented in two formats: in sections and complete. Where the reading is presented in sections, each segment is followed by questions on content and vocabulary. Where the reading is presented in its complete form, it is followed by questions on content that ask the reader for inferences, conclusions, opinions, and main ideas. With this dual format, the teacher and students have three choices: all the students may read the passage in segments, then read it in its entirety; all the students may read the passage completely first, then attend to the questions following each segment; or the students may each choose which format they prefer to read first, according to their own preferences and needs.

The exercises that follow the reading passage are intended to develop and improve reading proficiency (including the ability to learn new vocabulary from context) and comprehension of English sentence structure. The activities give students the opportunity to master useful vocabulary encountered in the articles through discussion and group work and lead the students to comprehension of main ideas and specific information.

Lower level language students need considerable visual reinforcement of ideas and vocabulary. Therefore, this text contains a great many illustrations. In addition, many of the follow-up activities are of the type that enable students to manipulate the information in the text and supplemental information. In fact, the teacher may want the students to use the blackboard to work on the charts and lists in the activities throughout the chapters.

Much of the vocabulary is recycled in the exercises and activities in any given chapter, as well as throughout the book. Experience has shown that beginning level students especially need repeated exposure to new vocabulary and word forms. Repetition of vocabulary in varied contexts helps the students not only understand the new vocabulary better, but also helps them remember it.

As the students work through the text, they will learn and improve reading skills and develop confidence in their growing English proficiency skills. At the same time, the teacher will be able to observe their steady progress towards skillful, independent reading.

Acknowledgements

We are grateful to everyone at Heinle & Heinle for their help and support. We thank the staff, faculty, and students at the English Language Institute at Queens College for their continuing interest and suggestions. A special thanks also goes to Richard Basch, Esq., for his good counsel.

L.C.S. and N.N.M.

Introduction

How to Use This Book

Every chapter in this book consists of the following:

Prereading Preparation
Reading Passage in Segments with Reading Analysis
Complete Reading Passage
Scanning for Information
Word Forms
Vocabulary in Context
Follow-up Activities
Topics for Discussion and Writing
Crossword Puzzle
Cloze Quiz

There is an Index of Key Words and Phrases and an Answer Key at the end of the book.

The format of each chapter in the book is consistent. Although each chapter can be done entirely in class, some exercises may be assigned for homework. This, of course, depends on the individual teacher's preference, as well as the availability of class time. Classwork will be most effective when done in pairs or groups, giving the students more opportunity to interact with the material and with each other.

Prereading Preparation

This prereading activity is designed to stimulate student interest and provide preliminary vocabulary for the passage itself. The importance of prereading preparation should not be underestimated. Studies have shown the positive effect of prereading preparation in motivating student interest and in enhancing reading comprehension. In fact, prereading discussion of topics and visuals has been shown to be more effective in improving reading comprehension than prereading vocabulary exercises per se. Time should be spent describing and discussing the illustrations as well as discussing the prereading questions. Furthermore, the students should try to relate the topic to their own experience, and try to predict what they are going to read about. Students may even choose to write a story based on the chapter opening illustration.

The Reading Passage with Reading Analysis

Each reading passage is presented in segments. As the students read the passage for the first time, they can focus on the meaning of each paragraph. This exercise requires the students to think about the meanings of words and phrases, the structure of sentences and paragraphs, and the relationships of ideas to each other. They also have the opportunity to think about and predict what they will read in the next paragraph of the reading. This exercise is very effective when done in groups. It may also be done individually, but it gives the students an excellent opportunity to discuss possible answers.

Reading Passage

Students should be instructed to read the entire passage carefully a second time and to pay attention to the main idea and important details.

Scanning for Information

After students have read the complete passage, they will read the questions in this exercise, scan the complete passage for the answers, and then write the answers in the spaces under each question. The last question in this section always refers to the main idea. When the students are finished, they may compare their answers with a classmate's. The pairs of students can then refer back to the passage and check their answers. The students may prefer to work in pairs throughout this exercise.

Word Forms

In order to successfully complete the word form exercises in this book, the students will need to understand parts of speech, specifically nouns, verbs, adjectives, and adverbs. Teachers should point out each word form's position in a sentence. Students will develop a sense for which part of speech is necessary in a given sentence. Because this is a low-level text, the Word Form exercise simply asks students to identify the correct part of speech. They do not need to consider the tense of verbs or the number (singular or plural) of nouns.

Vocabulary in Context

This is a fill-in exercise designed as a review of the items in the previous exercises. The vocabulary has been highlighted either in the prereading or elsewhere in the chapter. This exercise may be done for homework as a review or in class as group work.

Follow-up Activities

This section contains various activities appropriate to the information in the passages. Some activities are designed for pair and small group work.

Students are encouraged to use the information and vocabulary from the passages both orally and in writing. The teacher may also use these questions and activities as home or in-class assignments. Some follow-up activities help the students interact with the real world because they require the students to go outside the classroom to interview people or to get specific information. In this way, students are not limited to speaking, reading, or learning in the classroom.

Topics for Discussion and Writing

This section provides ideas or questions for the students to think about and/or work on alone, in pairs, or in small groups. It provides beginning students with writing opportunities appropriate for their ability level, usually at the paragraph level.

Crossword Puzzle

Each chapter contains a crossword puzzle based on the vocabulary used in that chapter. Crossword puzzles are especially effective when the students work in pairs. Working together provides students with an opportunity to speak together and to discuss their reasons for their answers.

If pronunciation practice of letters is needed, students can go over the puzzle orally: The teacher can have the students spell out their answers in addition to pronouncing the words themselves. Students invariably enjoy doing crossword puzzles. They are a fun way to reinforce the vocabulary presented in the various exercises in each chapter, and they require students to pay attention to correct spelling.

Cloze Quiz

The Cloze test is the passage itself with 10–20 vocabulary items focused on the previous exercises and question sections omitted. The Cloze quiz tests not only vocabulary but also sentence structure and comprehension in general. The students are given the words to be filled in the blank spaces.

Index of Key Words and Phrases

This section contains words and phrases from all the chapters for easy reference. It is located after the last chapter.

Answer Key

The Answer Key is located at the end of the book and provides the answers to the exercises.

Sea and Land Animals

Sharks:
Useful Hunters of the Sea

• Prereading Preparation

1. What do you know about sharks? Try to answer the following
   questions with your teacher and classmates. After you read the
   story, check your answers.

Questions	Answers
1. What are sharks?	1.
2. Where do sharks live?	2.
3. What do sharks eat?	3.
4. How do sharks hunt?	4. _____ a. by smell _____ b. by sound _____ c. by sight _____ d. a, b, and c
5. Are all sharks dangerous?	5.
6. How many kinds of sharks are there? (Write a number.)	6.

2. The title of this reading is "Sharks: Useful Hunters of the Sea."
   What will this story tell you? Read the following sentences.
   Check the information that you think you will read about.

   _____ a. Sharks kill people.
   _____ b. Sharks are very old animals.
   _____ c. Sharks are good hunters.
   _____ d. Sharks live a long time.
   _____ e. Sharks hunt boats and ships.

Directions: Read each paragraph carefully. Then answer the questions.

Sharks: Useful Hunters of the Sea

Most people are afraid of sharks, but they usually do not know very much about them. For example, there are 350 kinds of sharks, and all of them are meat eaters. Some sharks are very big. The whale shark is 50 to 60 feet long. But some sharks are very small. The dwarf shark is only 6 inches long.

1. How many different kinds of sharks are there?_____

2. _____ True   _____ False   All sharks are meat eaters.

3. _____ True   _____ False   All sharks are very big.

4. How big is the whale shark? _____

5. How big is the dwarf shark? _____

6. Many people are afraid of sharks because

   a. there are many kinds of sharks
   b. sharks are meat eaters
   c. some sharks are small and some sharks are big

Sharks are 100 million years old. In fact, they lived at the same time as dinosaurs. Today, sharks live in every ocean in the world, but most sharks live in warm water. They keep the oceans clean because they eat sick fish and animals. Most sharks have four to six rows of teeth. When a shark's tooth falls out, another tooth moves in from behind.

7. How old are sharks? _____

8. Where do most sharks live?

   a. in every ocean in the world
   b. in warm water

9. Sharks are important because

   a. they clean the ocean
   b. they are very big
   c. they eat fish

10. What happens when a shark's tooth falls out?

    a. It cannot eat.
    b. Another tooth moves in.
    c. The shark dies.

    Sharks do not have ears. However, they "hear" sounds and movements in the water. Any sound or movement makes the water vibrate. Sharks can feel these vibrations, and they help the sharks find food. Sharks use their large eyes to find food, too. Most sharks see best in low light. They often hunt for food at dawn, in the evening, or in the middle of the night.

11. _____ True _____ False Sharks have ears.

12. _____ True _____ False Sharks can feel movements in the
                                          water.

13. Sharks can find food because

    a. they feel vibrations
    b. they can see with their eyes
    c. both a and b

14. a. When do sharks hunt for food?

    _____

    b. Sharks hunt for food at these times because

        1. they are hungry at night
        2. they see well in low light
        3. other fish are sleeping

    c. **Dawn** is

        1. at night
        2. in the middle of the day
        3. early morning

Scientists want to learn more about sharks for several reasons. For example, cancer is common in many animals, including people. However, it is rare in sharks. Scientists want to find out why sharks almost never get cancer. Maybe this information can help people prevent cancer too.

15. **Rare** means

    a. common
    b. not common

16. _____ True _____ False Many sharks have cancer.

17. _____ True _____ False Many animals and humans have cancer.

18. Scientists want to find out

    a. why animals get cancer
    b. why sharks always get cancer
    c. why sharks almost never get cancer

19. Information about sharks may

    a. help people prevent cancer
    b. help animals prevent cancer
    c. help sharks live longer

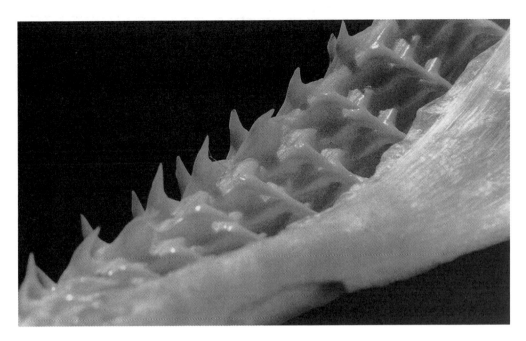

Directions: Read the complete passage. When you are finished, you will answer the questions that follow.

Sharks: Useful Hunters of the Sea

1   Most people are afraid of sharks, but they usually do not know
2 very much about them. For example, there are 350 kinds of sharks,
3 and all of them are meat eaters. Some sharks are very big. The
4 whale shark is 50 to 60 feet long. But some sharks are very small.
5 The dwarf shark is only 6 inches long. Sharks are 100 million years
6 old. In fact, they lived at the same time as dinosaurs. Today, sharks
7 live in every ocean in the world, but most sharks live in warm
8 water. They keep the oceans clean because they eat sick fish and
9 animals. Most sharks have four to six rows of teeth. When a shark's
10 tooth falls out another tooth moves in from behind. Sharks do not
11 have ears. However, they "hear" sounds and movements in the
12 water. Any sound or movement makes the water vibrate. Sharks can
13 feel these vibrations, and they help the sharks find food. Sharks use
14 their large eyes to find food, too. Most sharks see best in low light.
15 They often hunt for food at dawn, in the evening, or in the middle
16 of the night. Scientists want to learn more about sharks for several
17 reasons. For example, cancer is common in many animals, including
18 people. However, it is rare in sharks. Scientists want to find out
19 why sharks almost never get cancer. Maybe this information can
20 help people prevent cancer too.

• A. Scanning for Information

Read the following questions. Then go back to the complete passage and scan quickly for the answers. Write them in the space under each question.

1. a. What are two types of sharks?

   _____

   b. How are they different?

   _____

   c. How are they the same?

   _____

2. How do sharks keep the oceans clean?

   _____

3. How do sharks find food?

   _____

4. Why do scientists want to learn more about sharks?

   _____

5. What is the main idea of this passage?

   a. Sharks are dangerous.
   b. Sharks are important and useful animals.
   c. Sharks are meat eaters.

• B. Word Forms

In English, some words can be either a noun (n.) or a verb (v.), for example, *hunt*. Read the sentences below. Decide if the correct word is a noun or a verb. Circle your answer. Do the example below before you begin.

Example: a. Sharks <u>hunt/hunt</u> for food in low light.
(v.)   (n.)

b. This <u>hunt/ hunt</u> can be at night or at dawn.
(v.)   (n.)

1. Many animals <u>help/ help</u> scientists learn about cancer.
(v.)   (n.)

2. This <u>help/ help</u> can be important to people.
(v.)   (n.)

3. There are many <u>uses/ uses</u> for computers.
(v.)   (n.)

4. I <u>use/ use</u> my computer almost every day.
(v.) (n.)

5. Next month Marina will <u>move/ move</u> to Florida.
(v.)   (n.)

6. She is very excited about this <u>move/ move</u>.
(v.)   (n.)

7. My doorbell sometimes <u>sounds/ sounds</u> like my telephone.
(v.)   (n.)

8. These two <u>sounds/ sounds</u> are very similar.
(v.)   (n.)

• C. Vocabulary in Context

Read the following sentences. Choose the correct word for each sentence. Write your answer in the blank space.

common (adj.)   **rare** (adj.)   **afraid** (adj.)   **for example**

1. Cancer is _____ in many animals. These animals become very sick.

2. Many people are _____ of sharks. People think sharks will hurt them.

3. There are 350 different kinds of sharks. _____ , the whale shark is one kind.

4. Most sharks never get cancer. Cancer is very _____ in sharks.

another (adj.)   **hunt** (v.)   **movements** (n.)

5. Sharks have a lot of teeth. When a shark's tooth falls out, _____ tooth moves in.

6. Sharks can feel _____, or vibrations, in the water.

7. Sharks often _____ for food at night.

In fact   **prevent** (n.) **several** (adj.)

8. Scientists want to stop cancer in people, so they study sharks. Scientists want to _____ cancer in people.

9. Sharks hunt for food at _____ different times: at night, at dawn, and in the evening.

10. Sharks are very, very old. _____ , they are as old as dinosaurs.

• D. Follow-up Activities

1. The following chart shows where sharks live. Look at it carefully, and then answer the questions that follow.

   a. The _____ lives near the coast.

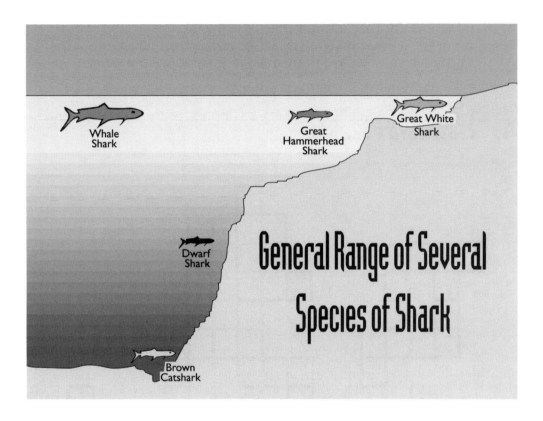

   b. The _____ lives near the surface of the oceans and seas.

   c. The _____ lives in very deep water.

   d. The _____ lives in deeper water than the great hammerhead shark.

2. Visit an aquarium. Spend some time watching a shark or other animal. Watch carefully how it moves and what it does. Draw a sketch of the animal. Then report back to your class. Show your sketch, and give a report of your observations.

• E.   Topics for Discussion and Writing

1. What information did you learn about sharks? Do not look back at the reading. Write five sentences about sharks. Put your sentences on the blackboard. Compare your information with your classmates' information. Did you all learn the same information?

2. Write about another animal that lives in the ocean, for example, an octopus, a sea turtle, a whale, or a dolphin. What does this animal look like? Where does it live? What does it eat?

F.   Crossword Puzzle

Crossword Puzzle Clues

Across

2. Sharks look for food during the day and at _____.
4. Sharks _____ very, very old animals.
7. _____ sharks are meat eaters.
9. Sharks have very good _____, so they can see very well.
11. Sharks live in every _____ and sea in the world.
12. Sharks _____ see very well.
15. Sharks feel _____ or vibrations in the water.
16. Most sharks are very big, but some sharks are very _____.
18. All sharks eat _____.
20. Most people are _____ of sharks. They do not like them.
21. Are there many kinds of sharks? _____, there are.
23. There are 350 _____ of sharks.
25. Most sharks like to live in _____ water, not cold water.

Down

1. Sharks are 100 _____ years old.
3. John is a scientist. _____ studies sharks.
5. Cancer is very _____ in sharks. They usually do not get cancer.
6. Sharks have large eyes. They can _____ in low light.
8. _____ are fish.
10. _____ are people who study sharks.
12. _____ is a serious illness.
13. Sharks do _____ have ears.
14. _____ sharks are fish.
17. There are _____ different kinds of sharks.
19. Scientists want _____ find out why sharks do not get cancer.
20. I _____ not afraid of sharks.
22. The whale shark is very _____. It is not small.
24. Early morning is _____.
26. I, _____; he, him; she, her

G. Cloze Quiz

Read the passage below. Fill in each space with the correct word from the list. Use each word only once.

afraid   lived   only   small   some

Most people are (1) _____ of sharks, but they usually do not know very much about them. (2) _____ sharks are very big. But some sharks are very (3) _____ . The dwarf shark is (4) _____ six inches long. Sharks are 100 million years old. In fact, they (5) _____ at the same time as dinosaurs.

another   eat   ocean   teeth   they

Sharks live in every (6) _____ in the world, but most sharks live in warm water. (7) _____ keep the oceans clean because they (8) _____ sick fish and animals. Most sharks have four to six rows of (9) _____ . When a shark's tooth falls out, (10) _____ tooth moves in from behind.

C·H·A·P·T·E·R 2

A Brief History of Horses with Humans

• Prereading Preparation

Work with a partner. Discuss the following questions.

1. What are some uses for horses?

   a. _____

   b. _____

   c. _____

   d. _____

2. Are horses important to people? Why or why not?

3. The title of this reading is "A Brief History of Horses with Humans." What will this story tell you? Read the following sentences. Check the information that you think you will read about.

   _____ a. Horses eat grass.

   _____ b. Horses live a long time.

   _____ c. People learned to use horses for work.

   _____ d. People hunted horses for food.

   _____ e. Horses are strong.

   _____ f. Horses are fast.

   _____ g. Horses are different colors.

Directions: Read each paragraph carefully. Then answer the questions

A Brief History of Horses with Humans

For many thousands of years, people hunted for horses to eat. In fact, horse meat was a very common food. Then, about 6,000 years ago, people discovered that horses were useful, too. Somewhere in southern Russia and west central Asia, people first began to use horses to work for them.

1. _____ True _____ False   For a long time, many people ate horse meat.

2. **Common** means

    a. usual
    b. not usual

3. When did people begin to use horses for work?_____

4. People first used horses for work

    a. all over the world
    b. in the United States
    c. in Russia and Asia

5. What do you think the next paragraph will discuss?

    a. the different things that people ate
    b. the different ways that people used horses
    c. the different history of Russia and Asia

This discovery changed human history. People were able to travel faster and farther with horses. They were able to leave their own land. Many people went to distant lands, met new people, and saw new places. They taught other people how to use horses. Then, about 3,500 years ago, people in Mesopotamia (modern Iraq) began to use horses to help them win wars against their enemies. They drove chariots, or carts, pulled by two or more horses. It was impossible for an enemy on foot to fight against a soldier in a chariot. As a result, armies with horses and chariots were very powerful. About 100 years later, men learned to ride on horses. These armies became even more powerful.

6. **This discovery** means

    a. people began to eat horses
    b. people started to use horses for work and travel
    c. people discovered where horses were

7. **People were able to travel faster and farther.** This sentence means

    a. people traveled more quickly
    b. people traveled to places far away
    c. both a and b

8. Many people went to distant lands, met new people and saw new places because

    a. there were many wars
    b. they traveled by horse
    c. they changed history

9. Where did people begin to use horses to fight wars?

    a. Russia
    b. Asia
    c. Mesopotamia

10. A **soldier** is

    a. a person in an army
    b. a person on a horse
    c. a person in a chariot

11. **An enemy on foot** is

    a. an enemy on a horse
    b. an enemy who is walking
    c. an enemy with two feet

12. **As a result** means

    a. so
    b. and
    c. but

13. When did men learn to ride on horses?

    a. about 100 years ago
    b. about 3,400 years ago
    c. about 3,500 years ago

14. These armies became even more powerful because

    a. the soldiers rode horses
    b. the horses pulled carts
    c. the enemies were afraid

For many centuries, until railroads were built, people everywhere depended on horses to work and to travel. In fact, horses worked to help build the roads and railroads we use today. They also worked on farms. They pulled fire engines and ambulances in cities. Horses were indispensable to people for a very long time.

15. What is a **century**?

    a. 10 years
    b. several years
    c. 100 years

16. What does **in fact** mean?

    a. really
    b. too
    c. but

17. **Until** means

    a. when something begins
    b. when something ends
    c. when something continues

18. _____True _____ False   People depended only on horses to work and travel after they built railroads.

19. _____True _____ False   Horses helped build the railroads.

20. **Indispensable** means

    a. everywhere
    b. fast
    c. necessary

Directions: Read the complete passage. When you are finished, you will answer the questions that follow.

A Brief History of Horses with Humans

1   For many thousands of years, people hunted for horses to
2 eat. In fact, horse meat was a very common food. Then, about
3 6,000 years ago, people discovered that horses were useful, too.
4 Somewhere in southern Russia and west central Asia, people first
5 began to use horses to work for them.
6   This discovery changed human history. People were able to
7 travel faster and farther with horses. They were able to leave
8 their own land. Many people went to distant lands, met new
9 people, and saw new places. They taught other people how to use
10 horses. Then, about 3,500 years ago, people in Mesopotamia
11 (modern Iraq) began to use horses to help them win wars against
12 their enemies. They drove chariots, or carts, pulled by two or
13 more horses. It was impossible for an enemy on foot to fight
14 against a soldier in a chariot. As a result, armies with horses
15 and chariots were very powerful. About 100 years later, men
16 learned to ride on horses. These armies became even more
17 powerful.
18   For many centuries, until railroads were built, people
19 everywhere depended on horses to work and to travel. In fact,
20 horses worked to help build the roads and railroads we use today.
21 They also worked on farms. They pulled fire engines and
22 ambulances in cities. Horses were indispensable to people for a
23 very long time.

• A. Scanning for Information

Read the following questions. Then go back to the complete passage and scan quickly for the answers. Write them in the space under each question.

1. a. When did people discover that horses were useful?

   _____

   b. Where did this discovery happen?

   _____

   c. What did these people use horses for?

   _____

2. Read line 6: **This discovery changed human history.** How?

   _____

   _____

3. How did horses help to win wars?

   _____

   _____

4. What were some uses for horses in the past?

   _____

5. The main idea of this passage is

   a. People discovered horses 6,000 years ago.
   b. For a long time, horses were very useful to people.
   c. Horses helped people win many wars against enemies.

• B. Word Forms

In English, some verbs (v.) become adjectives (adj.) when you add the suffix *-ful*, for example *thank* (v.), *thankful* (adj.).
　　Read the following sentences. Decide if the correct word is a verb or an adjective. Circle your answer. Do the example below before you begin.

Example: a. We usually <u>thank / thankful</u> a person who helps us.
　　　　　　　　　　(v.)　　　(adj.)

　　　　　b. We usually feel <u>thank / thankful</u> when someone helps us.
　　　　　　　　　　　　(v.)　　　(adj.)

1. People <u>use / useful</u> computers every day.
　　　　(v.)　　(adj.)

2. Computers are very <u>use / useful</u> .
　　　　　　　　　　(v.)　　(adj.)

3. This book is very <u>help / helpful</u> .
　　　　　　　　　(v.)　　(adj.)

4. This book <u>helps / helpful</u> us learn.
　　　　　(v.)　　　(adj.)

5. I am a <u>care / careful</u> driver.
　　　　(v.)　　　(adj.)

6. I <u>care / careful</u> about safety.
　　(v.)　　　(adj.)

• C. Vocabulary in Context

Read the following sentences. Choose the correct word for each sentence. Write your answer in the blank space.

begin (v.)   **travel** (v.)   **until** (prep.)

1. Every year, Leona and John _____ to a different country on their vacation.

2. Last night I studied at the library _____ it closed.

3. We always _____ our class at 9:30.

common (adj.)   **in fact**   **mean** (v.)

4. I don't understand "discuss." What does this word _____?

5. People depend on cars and airplanes. _____ , people cannot work or travel without them.

6. Hamburgers are a very _____ food in the United States. Many people eat them.

as a result   **brief** (adj.)   **indispensable** (adj.)

7. We need to write a _____ story—only one page.

8. Today, computers are _____ to many businesses, such as banks and schools.

9. Carol felt sick last night. _____ , she went to bed early.

• D. Follow-up Activities

1. Work alone or in a small group. Use the chart below to make a
   list of other animals that are useful to people. Describe the
   ways each animal has helped people.

Animal	Ways This Animal is Useful
dog	
camel	
elephant	
goat	

2. Today we have many machines and appliances to help us complete different tasks. Some of these conveniences are listed below. Describe what people use each item for today, and then tell what people used in the past for the same purpose.

Modern Machine or Appliance	Uses for the Machine or Appliance Today	What People Used in the Past
telephone		
refrigerator		
stove		
computer		
electric lights		
washing machine		
clocks and watches		
photocopy machine		
elevator		

• E. Topics for Discussion and Writing

1. Work alone or with a partner. Describe an ancient discovery that changed history. Make a list of all the discoveries on the blackboard. Discuss the discoveries with your classmates, and then put them in order of importance. In other words, the discovery you think is the most important is number 1. The discovery you think is the least important is number 10.

1. _____

2. _____

3. _____

4. _____

5. _____

6. _____

7. _____

8. _____

9. _____

10. _____

2. Write a paragraph. Describe your favorite animal. What does it look like? Where does it live? Why do you like it?

F. Crossword Puzzle

Crossword Puzzle Clues

Across

1. Thousands of years ago, people used horses for _____. They ate horses.
2. Thousands of years ago, horse meat was a very _____ food.
5. Today, _____ is the name of Mesopotamia.
7. Far away.
8. Horses were _____ to people for thousands of years. People needed horses very much.
10. Horse _____ is not a usual food today.
11. Thousands _____ years ago, people lived very differently.
13. Horses helped to _____ roads.
14. People _____ horses for food.
16. Horses are _____ animals. They are very strong.
18. People needed horses to work. In _____, people were not able to travel far without them.

Down

1. Some soldiers rode horses. Other soldiers traveled on _____.
2. Soldiers drove _____, or carts, pulled by horses.
3. One hundred years ago, horses pulled _____ engines and ambulances.
4. Our class begins _____ 10 o'clock.
6. Short; not long.
7. People _____ on horses. They needed horses.
9. 3,500 years ago, people had horses in their _____ to help them win wars.
10. Airplanes are a kind of _____ transportation.
12. Many _____ traveled to distant places after they began to use horses for work.
15. Horses are very _____ animals. They can do different kinds of work.
17. Mary and I study every day. _____ do our homework in the library.
19. I _____ ride a horse. Can you?

G. Cloze Quiz

Read the following passage. Fill in each space with the correct word from the list. Use each word only once.

first   food   hunted   people   useful

For many thousands of years, people (1)_____ for horses to eat. In fact, horse meat was a very common (2)_____. Then, about 6,000 years ago, (3)_____ discovered that horses were (4)_____ , too. Somewhere in southern Russia and west central Asia, people (5)_____ began to use horses to work for them.

depended   fact   indispensable   railroads   worked

For many centuries, until railroads were built, people everywhere (6)_____ on horses to work and to travel. In (7)_____, horses worked to help build the roads and (8)_____we use today. They also (9)_____ on farms. They pulled fire engines and ambulances. Horses were (10)_____ to people for a very long time.

Language and Culture

C·H·A·P·T·E·R 3

Learning a Second Language

• Prereading Preparation

1. Work with a partner. Make a list of things you can do that will help you learn a second language.

Things We Can Do to Help Ourselves Learn a Second Language

1.	
2.	
3.	
4.	
5.	

2. Compare your list with your other classmates' lists. What can you add to your list?

_____

_____

_____

_____

3. Read the title of this chapter. What will this passage discuss?

_____

Directions: Read each paragraph carefully. Then answer the questions.

Learning a Second Language

   Some people learn a second language easily. Other people have trouble learning a new language. How can you help yourself learn a new language, such as English? There are several ways to make learning English a little easier and more interesting.

1. _____ True _____ False Everyone learns a second language easily.

2. Other people have **trouble** learning a new language.

   Trouble means

   a. difficulty
   b. classes
   c. reasons

3. **Several** means

   a. easier
   b. many
   c. different

4. What do you think the next paragraph will discuss?

   a. problems learning a new language
   b. ways to learn a new language more easily
   c. where to study a second language

The first step is to feel positive about learning English. If you believe that you can learn, you will learn. Be patient. You do not have to understand everything all at once. It is natural to make mistakes when you learn something new. We can learn from our mistakes. In other words, do not worry about taking risks.

5. What does it mean to feel positive about learning English?

   a. If you believe you can learn, you will learn.
   b. You can understand everything all at once.
   c. You must make mistakes.

6. When you are **patient**, do you worry about learning English very quickly?

   a. Yes
   b. No

7. You do not have to understand everything **all at once.**

   All at once means

   a. slowly
   b. easily
   c. right now

8. We can learn from our mistakes. **In other words**, do not worry about **taking risks**.

   a. What follows **in other words**?
      1. an opposite idea
      2. an example
      3. the same idea

   b. **Taking risks** means
      1. taking chances
      2. working hard
      3. feeling positive

9. What do you think the next paragraph will discuss?

   a. different kinds of languages
   b. making mistakes
   c. the second step

The second step is to practice your English. For example, write in a journal, or diary, every day. You will get used to writing in English, and you will feel comfortable expressing your ideas in English. After several weeks, you will see that your writing is improving. In addition, you must speak English every day. You can practice with your classmates outside class. You will all make mistakes, but gradually you will become comfortable communicating in English.

10. What is a **journal**?

    a. a diary
    b. practice
    c. an example

11. How can you practice your English?

    a. Write in a journal every day.
    b. Practice with your classmates after class.
    c. Both a and b

12. **After several weeks** means

    a. after a few days
    b. when a few weeks are finished
    c. a week later

13. What follows **in addition**?

    a. more information
    b. the same information
    c. the result

14. **Gradually** means

    a. quickly
    b. carefully
    c. slowly

15. **Communicating** in English means

    a. speaking and listening
    b. reading
    c. studying

16. What will the next paragraph discuss?

    a. making mistakes
    b. feeling comfortable
    c. the third step

The third step is to keep a record of your language learning. You can write this in your journal. After each class, think about what you did. Did you answer a question correctly? Did you understand something the teacher explained? Perhaps the lesson was difficult, but you tried to understand it. Write these accomplishments in your journal.

17. When you **keep a record** of something,

    a. you write it on paper
    b. you remember it
    c. you tell someone

18. _____ True _____ False   You can keep a record of your language learning in your journal.

19. **Perhaps** means

    a. usually
    b. sometimes
    c. maybe

20. **Accomplishments** are

    a. successes
    b. mistakes
    c. lessons

You must be positive about learning English and believe that you can do it. It is important to practice every day and make a record of your achievements. You will enjoy learning English, and you will feel more confidence in yourself.

21. **Achievements** are

    a. accomplishments
    b. lessons
    c. problems

22. Read the following actions. Which ones are accomplishments?

_____ a. You asked a question in class.

_____ b. You brought a notebook and a pen to class.

_____ c. You made a mistake, but you understood why.

_____ d. You tried to answer a question.

_____ e. You spoke your native language to a classmate.

Directions: Read the complete passage. When you are finished, you will answer the questions that follow.

Learning a Second Language

1   Some people learn a second language easily. Other people have
2 trouble learning a new language. How can you help yourself learn a
3 new language, such as English? There are several ways to make
4 learning English a little easier and more interesting.

5   The first step is to feel positive about learning English. If you
6 believe that you can learn, you will learn. Be patient. You do not
7 have to understand everything all at once. It is natural to make
8 mistakes when you learn something new. We can learn from our
9 mistakes. In other words, do not worry about taking risks.

10   The second step is to practice your English. For example, write in
11 a journal, or diary, every day. You will get used to writing in English,
12 and you will feel comfortable expressing your ideas in English. After
13 several weeks, you will see that your writing is improving. In
14 addition, you must speak English every day. You can practice with
15 your classmates outside class. You will all make mistakes, but
16 gradually you will become comfortable communicating in English.

17 The third step is to keep a record of your language learning. You
18 can write this in your journal. After each class, think about what
19 you did. Did you answer a question correctly? Did you understand
20 something the teacher explained? Perhaps the lesson was difficult,
21 but you tried to understand it. Write these accomplishments in your
22 journal.
23 You must be positive about learning English and believe that you
24 can do it. It is important to practice every day and make a record of
25 your achievements. You will enjoy learning English, and you will
26 feel more confidence in yourself.

• A. Scanning for Information

Read the following questions. Then go back to the complete passage
and scan quickly for the answers. Write them in the space under each
question.

1. Are there ways to make learning a second language easier?

   a. Yes
   b. No

2. How many steps are there? _____

3. Describe each step. Then give one example of each step.

   a. _____

   _____

   b. _____

   _____

   c. _____

   _____

4. What is the main idea of this passage?

   a. It is very important to learn a second language.
   b. Some people learn a second language easily. Other people
      do not.
   c. There are ways to help you learn a second language more
      easily.

• B. Word Forms

In English, some adjectives (adj.) become adverbs (adv.) by adding the suffix *-ly*, for example *brief* (adj.), *briefly* (adv.).
    Read the following sentences. Decide if the correct word is an adjective or an adverb. Circle your answer. Do the example before you begin.

Example: a. John spoke very <u>brief / briefly</u> at the meeting.
                         (adj.)   (adv.)

            b. John gave a very <u>brief / briefly</u> speech because he had
                              (adj.)   (adv.)

        to leave early.

 1. This is an <u>easy / easily</u> exercise.
        (adj.)   (adv.)

 2. I can write the answers <u>easy / easily</u> .
                         (adj.)   (adv.)

 3. Many people can speak a second language very <u>natural / naturally</u>.
                                              (adj.)   (adv.)

 4. Children are <u>natural / naturally</u> language learners.
        (adj.)   (adv.)

 5. What is the <u>correct / correctly</u> answer?
        (adj.)   (adv.)

 6. The students answered the question <u>correct / correctly</u> .
                                 (adj.)   (adv.)

 7. Every day our English <u>gradual / gradually</u> improves.
                      (adj.)   (adv.)

 8. This <u>gradual / gradually</u> improvement is exciting.
        (adj.)   (adv.)

• C. Vocabulary in Context

Read the following sentences. Choose the correct word for each sentence. Write your answer in the blank space.

all at once   patient (adj.)   **risks** (n.)

1. Alice enjoys trying new, exciting activities. She really likes to take _____.

2. You can't learn how to use a computer _____. It takes time to learn everything you need to know.

3. My mother is a very _____ person. She always takes her time and is never in a hurry to finish something.

gradual (adj.)   **in other words**   **positive** (adj.)

4. Clark played the violin every day for four months. He saw a _____ improvement in his music.

5. I will take a math test tomorrow. I have studied hard, so I feel very _____ about the test.

6. Lucy eats fresh fruit and vegetables every day. She exercises five times a week, and she sleeps eight hours a night. _____, Lucy has a very healthy life.

confidence (n.) **in addition** **perhaps** (adv.) **trouble** (n.)

7. John is very tired today. _____ he didn't sleep well last night. I'll ask him.

8. We didn't take care of our car. Last week we went on vacation, and we had _____ with our car.

9. Tony needs to have more _____ . He is always afraid of doing something wrong.

10. Peter went to the store. He bought milk, meat, bread, and fruit. _____ , he got coffee and tea.

• D. Follow-up Activities

1. What is the most difficult part of learning English for you? Talk to several of your classmates. Ask them for suggestions to help you. Talk to several people outside your class. Ask them for suggestions, too. Try some of these suggestions, and then report back to your classmates. Tell them which suggestions were the most helpful and explain why.

2. Refer back to your list of things you can do to help yourself learn a language. Work with a partner. Talk about your lists. Decide when you can do these activities, and which language skills each activity will help you develop. Write them in the chart on the next page. There is an example to help you.

Activity	Skill (listening, speaking, reading, writing)	Place I Can Do This Activity
I ask questions when I don't understand.	speaking and listening	in class; in stores; on the street; at a train station or a bus stop; on the telephone

• E. Topics for Discussion and Writing

1. Start a journal of your language learning. Use a small notebook that will be easy to carry with you. Write in your journal several times a week. Write about your language learning accomplish-ments. In addition, describe the experiences you have with English. For example, when do you use English the most? When is it most difficult to practice English? Describe the ways you try to overcome these difficulties.

2. Imagine that you have a friend who plans to come to the United States to study English. Write a letter to your friend. Tell your friend what to expect. Give your friend advice about learning English more easily.

• F. Crossword Puzzle

Crossword Puzzle Clues

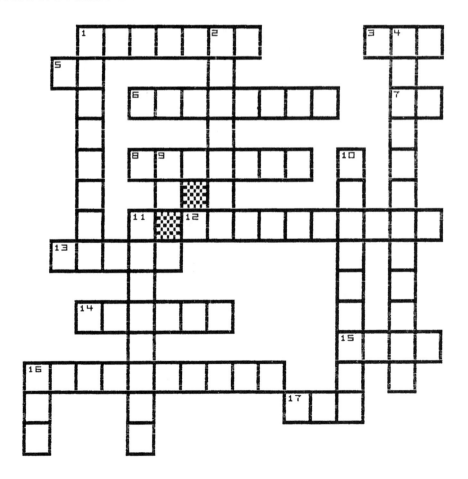

Across
1. When you study English, be _____ because learning a second language takes time.
3. English _____ many irregular verbs.
5. Is learning English easy? _____, it isn't.
6. We always make _____, or errors, when we learn something new.
7. **She, _____, it**
8. A _____ is a diary.
12. Your _____ are the other students in your class.
13. It takes time to _____ a second language.
14. Keep a _____ of your language learning in your diary.
15. Class begins at 9 o'clock. If you arrive after 9, you are _____.
16. Keep a diary and write your language learning achievements. This will give you _____.
17. Most students _____ that it is difficult to learn a second language.

Down
1. You need to feel very _____ about learning English. You need to say that you can do it!
2. It is _____, or normal, to make errors when you learn a second language.
4. Your _____, or accomplishments, will help you feel more comfortable.
9. Your pen is _____ your desk.
10. Slowly; after a long time
11. It is important to _____ English every day.
16. You _____ learn English!

• G. Cloze Quiz

Read the following passage. Fill in each space with the correct word from the list. Use each word only once.

easily   interesting   learn   such   trouble

Some people learn a second language (1)_____.
Other people have (2)_____ learning a new language.
How can you help yourself (3)_____ a new language,
(4)_____ as English? There are several ways to make
learning English, a little easier and more (5)_____ .

achievements   believe   confidence   positive   practice

You must be (6)_____ about learning English,
and you must (7)_____ that you can do it. It is
important to (8)_____ every day and make a
record of all your (9)_____ . You will enjoy
learning English, and you will feel more (10)_____
in yourself.

C·H·A·P·T·E·R

4

Food and Culture

• Prereading Preparation

1. What kind of food do you like to eat? For example, do you like American food, Korean food, Mexican food, etc.?

2. Does everyone like to eat the same food? Why or why not?

3. Work together with your classmates in small groups. Talk about food. First, write each student's name and country below. What food does each student prefer? Give examples of the kinds of food each student likes. Write your answers below.

Name	Country	Example of Food

4. Look at your list. What do you notice about the types of food each student likes?

5. With your group, write a definition, or explanation, of **culture**. Write your definition on the blackboard. Compare it with your classmates' definitions. What does **culture** mean?

6. The title of this article is "Food and Culture." What do you think this reading will discuss?

_____ a. All people like to eat the same kinds of food.

_____ b. Most people like to eat food from their own culture.

_____ c. Most people like to eat food from other cultures.

_____ d. Everyone thinks that the same kinds of food are good to eat.

_____ e. Not everyone thinks that the same kinds of food are good to eat.

_____ f. We all like some kinds of food because we always eat these kinds of food.

_____ g. We don't like some kinds of food because they are strange to us.

Directions: Read each paragraph carefully. Then answer the questions.

Food and Culture

What kind of food do you like to eat? Do you eat raw fish? dog meat? cheese? Many people prefer to eat food from their own culture. In other words, they like to eat food that they are familiar with.

Some people dislike certain food because they are not accustomed to it. The Japanese enjoy eating raw horse meat, but few Americans would want to taste it. Many Asians strongly dislike pizza, which is a very popular food in the United States. Milk is a very common drink in the United States for all people, young and old. In contrast, only babies drink milk in China.

1. Many people prefer to eat food from their own culture. **In other words**, they like to eat food that they are familiar with.

   a. These two sentences
      1. have opposite meanings
      2. have the same meanings
      3. are examples of each other

   b. **In other words**
      1. explains the first sentence
      2. gives an example
      3. shows a contrast

2. When a person is **accustomed to** something, it means that

   a. the person is familiar with it
   b. the person eats it
   c. the person dislikes it

3. The Japanese probably enjoy eating horse meat because

   a. it tastes good
   b. they are accustomed to it
   c. they dislike certain food

4. **Few** Americans would want to **taste** raw horse meat.

    a. **Few** Americans are
      1. many
      2. some
      3. not many

    b. In this sentence, **taste** means
      1. delicious
      2. flavor
      3. try

5. _____ True _____ False   Many Americans dislike pizza.

6. _____ True _____ False   Only babies drink milk in the United States.

7. **Strongly** means

    a. really
    b. sometimes
    c. carefully

8. **In contrast** shows

    a. a similarity
    b. an example
    c. a difference

Some people do not eat particular food for religious reasons. For instance, Hindus do not eat beef because cows are considered sacred. Jewish people and Moslems do not eat pork because pigs are thought to be unclean.

Sociologists say that people prefer the food that they grew up with. As a cultural group, we learn to like what is available to us. This is why in Africa some people eat termites, in Asia some people eat dog meat, and in Europe some people eat blood sausages.

9. **For instance** means

    a. because
    b. as a result
    c. for example

10. _____ True _____ False   Hindus do not eat beef for religious reasons.

11. Why don't Jewish people and Moslems eat pork?

    a. They don't like it.
    b. They believe that pigs are unclean.
    c. They do not have pigs in their countries.

12. What do you think a **sociologist** is?

_____

13. **We learn to like what is available to us.** What are some examples from the reading?

    a. _____

    b. _____

    c. _____

14. What do you think a **cultural group** is?

_____

Sometimes we need to change our eating habits. If we move or travel to a new place with a different culture, our favorite meat, fruit, and vegetables may not be available to us. As a result, we have to eat food that is different from the food we are used to. Slowly, this strange food becomes familiar to us. Our tastes change, and we begin to enjoy eating the food that used to seem unusual to us.

15. Why might we need to change our eating habits?

   _____

   _____

16. _____ True _____ False   When we eat food that is new to us, we may slowly become accustomed to it.

17. _____ True _____ False   We are never able to enjoy unusual food.

18. **Slowly** means

   a. gradually
   b. correctly
   c. quickly

19. **Our tastes change.** In this sentence, **tastes** means

   a. delicious
   b. preferences
   c. try

Directions: Read the complete passage. When you are finished, answer the questions that follow.

Food and Culture

1   What kind of food do you like to eat? Do you eat raw fish?
2 Dog meat? Cheese? Many people prefer to eat food from their own
3 culture. In other words, they like to eat food that they are
4 familiar with.
5   Some people dislike certain food because they are not
6 accustomed to it. The Japanese enjoy eating raw horse meat, but
7 few Americans would want to taste it. Many Asians strongly
8 dislike pizza, which is a very popular food in the United States.
9 Milk is a very common drink in the United States for all people,
10 young and old. In contrast, only babies drink milk in China.
11   Some people do not eat particular food for religious
12 reasons. For instance, Hindus do not eat beef because cows are
13 considered sacred. Jewish people and Moslems do not eat pork
14 because pigs are thought to be unclean.
15   Sociologists say that people prefer the food that they grew
16 up with. As a cultural group, we learn to like what is available
17 to us. This is why in Africa some people eat termites, in Asia

18 some people eat dog meat, and in Europe some people eat blood
19 sausages.
20   Sometimes we need to change our eating habits. If we move
21 or travel to a new place with a different culture, our favorite
22 meat, fruit, and vegetables may not be available to us. As a
23 result, we have to eat food that is different from the food we
24 are used to. Slowly, this strange food becomes familiar to us.
25 Our tastes change, and we begin to enjoy eating the food that used
26 to seem unusual to us.

• A. Scanning for Information

Read the following questions. Then go back to the complete passage
and scan quickly for the answers. Write them in the space under each
question.

  1. What kind of food do most people like to eat?

     _____

  2. Why do people dislike certain food?

     _____

  3. What are some examples of religious reasons why people do
     not eat certain food?

     _____

     _____

  4. In Africa some people eat termites, in Asia some people eat dog
     meat, and in Europe some people eat blood sausages. Why?

     _____

  5. What is the main idea of this passage?

     a. The food we like is a result of our cultural group.
     b. Asian people strongly dislike pizza.
     c. It is possible to change our eating habits.

• B. Word Forms

In English, some words can be either nouns (n.) or verbs (v.), for example, *light.* Read the following sentences Decide if the correct word is a noun or a verb. Circle your answer. Do the example below before you begin.

Example: a. Bob has many bright <u>lights</u> in his house.

(n. or v.)

b. Bob always <u>lights</u> them when he gets home in the

(n. or v.)

evening.

1. I enjoy the different <u>tastes</u> of fresh fruit.
(n. or v.)

2. Fruit always <u>tastes</u> delicious to me.
(n. or v.)

3. Carmen <u>moved</u> to California last summer.
(n. or v.)

4. It was an exciting <u>move</u>.
(n. or v.)

5. I'm very thirsty. May I have a cold <u>drink</u>?
(n. or v.)

6. I always <u>drink</u> water when I am thirsty.
(n. or v.)

7. Every semester the students <u>change</u> their class.
(n. or v.)

8. This <u>change</u> is very interesting for them.
(n. or v.)

• C. Vocabulary in Context

Read the following sentences. Choose the correct word for each sentence. Write your answer in the blank space.

for instance   in contrast   popular (adj.)

1. Steven loves all kinds of fruit. _____ , he enjoys apples, bananas, and grapes.

2. Ice cream is a _____ dessert. Many people eat it.

3. I don't eat eggs. _____ , my sister eats an egg for breakfast every day.

common (adj.)   **few** (adj.)   **in other words   prefers** (v.)

4. Kim _____ to eat Korean food. She doesn't really like American food.

5. Luis comes to class every day, always does his homework, and studies hard. _____ , Luis is a very good student.

6. Cereal is a _____ breakfast food in the United States. Many Americans eat it every day.

7. Milk is usually for children in China. _____ adults drink milk there.

accustomed to (v.)   **strongly** (adv.)   **unusual** (adj.)

8. When I first came to the United States, I did not like American food. Now I am _____ it. I enjoy American food.

9. Raw horse meat is an _____ food in the United States. Almost no one eats it.

10. Murat _____ dislikes Mexican food. He thinks it tastes too spicy.

• D. Follow-up Activities

1. This chapter talks about food and culture. It also tells us that sometimes our taste, or preference, for food can change. Is your taste in food now different from your taste in the past? What different food do you want to try in the future? Work with three partners. Discuss your ideas, and write them below.

Food I Liked in the Past	Food I Like Now	Food I Want to Try in the Future
1.	1.	1.
2.	2.	2.
3.	3.	3.
4.	4.	4.

2. As a class, combine your lists of food you like now and food you want to try in the future. Which type of food is the most popular among your classmates? Which type of food do most of your classmates want to try in the future? In your city, where can you go to try these different types of food?

3. Alone, or with your classmates, go to a restaurant that serves a kind of food you have never eaten before. Eat lunch or dinner there. Discuss the food with your classmates. Report back to your class. Describe the food you ate and why you liked it or didn't like it.

• E. Topics for Discussion and Writing

1. Go to a supermarket. Write a paragraph about the supermarket. How is it similar to food stores in your country? How is it different? Share your paragraph with your classmates. What did you notice that your classmates didn't? What did your classmates observe that you didn't?

2. Write in your journal. Describe your experience eating food from a different culture. Was it a positive experience? Why or why not? Share your experience with your classmates. Whose experience is the most interesting?

• F. Crossword Puzzle

• Crossword Puzzle Clues

Across

3. It is _____, or usual, for different people to like different kinds of food.

4. Americans usually eat three times a day: at breakfast, at _____, and at dinner.

7. Some people _____ dislike certain food and will not eat it.

10. What kind _____ food do people eat in your country?

13. There are many _____ why people do not eat certain food.

14. We become _____ to certain food because we grow up eating it.

15. We all _____ kinds of food that we like and don't like.

17. The food we like to eat depends on the _____ and the country we live in.

18. When we _____ to another country, we learn about different kinds of food.

19. Beef is not acceptable _____ for Hindus.

21. When we have to eat food that is different, we _____ become accustomed to it. It takes time.

23. We like to eat what we _____ used to eating.

24. Many people eat the food that is _____ to them. It is easy to get.

25. Most people _____ the food from their own culture and enjoy eating it.

Down

1. Sometimes people do _____ like food that looks or smells different.

2. Pizza is very _____ in the United States. Most people like it.

5. In China, it is very _____ for adults to drink milk. Only babies drink milk there.

6. When we _____ our eating habits, we learn to like different kinds of food.

8. Some people do not like the _____ of certain food, even when it looks amd smells good.

9. In every culture, people eat certain kinds of food _____ special holidays.

11. We usually like food that is _____ to us. We like food that we are used to.

12. Some people do not eat certain food for _____ reasons.

16. We _____ to eat food we are used to. We want to eat food we are accustomed to.

17. In Asia, some people eat dog meat. In _____, in the United States, no one eats dog meat.

20. The food that some people enjoy eating, other people _____ very much.

22. Is there any food that most people like to eat? _____, there is.

24. Each; every

• G. Close Quiz

Read the following passages. Fill in each space with the correct word from the list. Use each word only once.

accustomed   contrast   drink   popular   taste

Some people dislike certain food because they are not (1)_____ to it. The Japanese enjoy eating raw horse meat, but few Americans would want to (2)_____ it. Many Asians strongly dislike pizza, which is a very (3) _____ food in the United States. Milk is a very common (4)_____ in the United States for all people, young and old. In (5) _____, only babies drink milk in China.

different   enjoy   familiar   habits   result

Sometimes we need to change our eating (6)_____ . If we move or travel to a new place with a (7)_____ culture, our favorite meat, fruit, and vegetables may not be available to us. As a (8)_____ , we have to eat food that is different from the food we are used to. Slowly, this strange food becomes (9)_____ to us. Our tastes change, and we begin to (10)_____ eating the food that used to seem unusual to us.

Exercise and Fitness

The Importance of Exercise
for Children

• Prereading Preparation

1. Describe the illustration on the left. What are the children doing?

2. Work with a partner from another country. Discuss the questions in the information chart, and fill in the answers.

What Country are you from?	Do children exercise in school?	How often do children excercise in school?	What kinds of exercise do the children do?
1.			
2.			

3. Read the title of this passage. What do you think the reading will discuss?

Directions: Read each paragraph carefully. Then answer the questions.

The Importance of Exercise for Children

Joseph is a very busy 8-year-old boy. In the fall, he plays on a roller hockey team. He practices every Tuesday and Thursday after-noon and has a roller hockey game every Sunday morning. In the win-ter, Joseph plays basketball. His team practices one evening a week. They have a basketball game every Saturday morning. In the spring and summer, Joseph plays baseball. His team has a game twice a week and practices at least once. It is easy to see that Joseph is very active <u>after</u> school.

1. Why is Joseph **a very busy 8-year-old boy**?

    a. He goes to school a lot.
    b. He plays many different sports.
    c. He plays on a roller hockey team.

2. **His team practices one evening a week.** This means

    a. every night during the week
    b. at 1:00 during the week
    c. one night every week

3. Why is **after** underlined?

    a. for emphasis
    b. because it is a new word
    c. to show a contrast

4. What do you think the next paragraph will discuss?

    _____

In contrast, while most American children are <u>in</u> school, they have a physical education class just once a week for 45 minutes. Boys and girls from kindergarten to grade 12 do not have to have a physical education class in school every day. They do not have to exercise.

Not all American children are as active in sports after school as Joseph is. Therefore, these boys and girls need to exercise in school. Many people believe that the fitness and health of American children are in trouble. In fact, forty percent of children age 5 to 8 may be unhealthy already. For example, many have high blood pressure, are overweight, or have high cholesterol. Doctors believe that these conditions are the result of physical inactivity and poor diet.

5. **In contrast** shows

    a. an example
    b. a similarity
    c. a difference

6. What is a **physical education class**?

    a. a science class
    b. an exercise class
    c. an outdoor class

7. How often do most American children exercise in school?

   _____

8. _____ True _____ False   Most schoolchildren have a physical education class every day in the United States.

9. Not all American children are as active in sports after school as Joseph is. **Therefore,** these boys and girls need to exercise in school.

    a. The first sentence means that most American children
       1. are also very active in sports, like Joseph
       2. are more active in sports than Joseph is
       3. are less active in sports than Joseph is

    b. **Therefore** means

       1. also
       2. as a result
       3. for example

10. Many people believe that the **fitness** and health of American children are in trouble.

    a. **Fitness** means
       1. good physical condition
       2. exercise
       3. sports

    b. Many people believe that the fitness and health of American children
       1. are in America
       2. are interesting
       3. are a problem

11. _____ True _____ False   Many American children may be unhealthy already.

12. Doctors believe that these conditions are the result of **physical inactivity** and poor diet.

    What is **physical inactivity**?
    a. sports
    b. no exercise
    c. high blood pressure

In many countries in the world, all schoolchildren have to do one hour of exercise every day. These exercises do not have to be team sports. They may be simple, such as running, jumping, or climbing ropes. Doctors believe that habits learned early are more likely to stay with us through life. School is the perfect place to learn these habits, or practices. Active, healthy children who exercise regularly can become active, healthy adults.

13. _____ True _____ False   Running, jumping, and climbing ropes are always team sports.

14. Doctors believe that **habits** learned early are more likely to **stay with us through life**. School is the perfect place to learn these habits, or practices.

    a. **Habits** are

        1. places
        2. sports
        3. practices

    b. What kind of **habits** are these?

        1. reading habits
        2. exercise habits
        3. study habits

    c. **Stay with us through life** means

        1. we will continue to do it
        2. we will start these habits early
        3. we will not change

15. _____ True _____ False   The author believes that American children need to exercise in school more often.

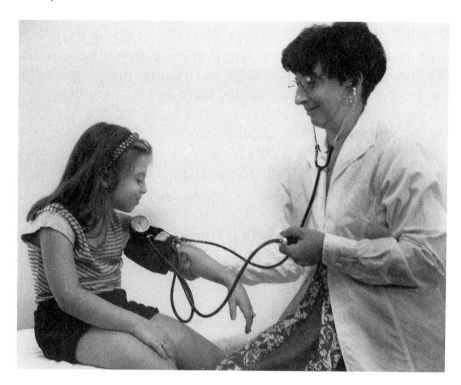

Directions: Read the complete passage. When you are finished, you will answer the questions that follow.

The Importance of Exercise for Children

1   Joseph is a very busy 8-year-old boy. In the fall, he plays on a
2 roller hockey team. He practices every Tuesday and Thursday
3 afternoon and has a roller hockey game every Sunday morning. In
4 the winter, Joseph plays basketball. His team practices one evening
5 a week. They have a basketball game every Saturday morning. In
6 the spring and summer, Joseph plays baseball. His team has a game
7 twice a week and practices at least once. It is easy to see that
8 Joseph is very active <u>after</u> school.
9   In contrast, while most American children are <u>in</u> school, they
10 have a physical education class just once a week for 45 minutes.
11 Boys and girls from kindergarten to grade 12 do not have to have a
12 physical education class in school every day. They do not have to
13 exercise.
14   Not all American children are as active in sports after school as
15 Joseph is. Therefore, these boys and girls need to exercise in
16 school. Many people believe that the fitness and health of
17 American children are in trouble. In fact, forty percent of children
18 age 5 to 8 may be unhealthy already. For example, many have high
19 blood pressure, are overweight, or have high cholesterol. Doctors

20 believe that these conditions are the result of physical inactivity
21 and poor diet.
22   In many countries in the world, all schoolchildren have to do
23 one hour of exercise every day. These exercises do not have to be
24 team sports. They may be simple, such as running, jumping, or
25 climbing ropes. Doctors believe that habits learned early are more
26 likely to stay with us through life. School is the perfect place to
27 learn these habits, or practices. Active, healthy children who
28 exercise regularly can become active, healthy adults.

• A. Scanning for Information

Read the following questions. Then go back to the complete passage
and scan quickly for the answers. Write them in the space under each
question.

1. What sports does Joseph play after school?

   _____

   _____

2. How often do most American children exercise <u>in</u> school?

   _____

   _____

3. a. Is physical activity important for children? _____

   b. What can happen when children do not exercise?

   _____

4. Active, healthy children who exercise regularly can become
   active, healthy adults. Why?

   a. because they were healthy children
   b. because they practiced many sports
   c. because they will continue their healthy habits

5. What is the main idea of this passage?

   a. Joseph does not exercise in school.
   b. Schoolchildren around the world exercise every day.
   c. It is very important for children to exercise in school.

• B. Word Forms

In English, some words can be either nouns (n.) or verbs (v.), for example, *drink*.

Read the following sentences. Decide if the correct word is a noun or a verb. Circle your answer. Do the example before you begin.

Example: a. I always <u>drink</u> water when I exercise.

(n. or v.)

b. This <u>drink</u> is very cold.

(n. or v.)

1. Liz <u>practices</u> the piano for one hour every day.
   (n. or v.)

2. Piano <u>practice</u> is fun for her.
   (n. or v.)

3. <u>Exercise</u> is important to our health.
   (n. or v.)

4. We <u>exercise</u> every afternoon.
   (n. or v.)

5. I sometimes <u>diet</u> to lose weight.
   (n. or v.)

6. My <u>diet</u> includes a lot of fruit and vegetables.
   (n. or v.)

7. Tom made many <u>changes</u> in his lifestyle.
   (n. or v.)

8. Tom also <u>changed</u> his eating habits.
   (n. or v.)

• C. Vocabulary in Context

Read the following sentences. Choose the correct answer for each sentence. Write your answer in the blank space.

at least   habit (n.)   **in contrast**

1. I try to eat _____ two pieces of fruit every day. I always eat an apple and a banana. Sometimes I eat an orange, too.

2. It is a good _____ to exercise three times a week. I usually exercise on Mondays, Thursdays, and Saturdays.

3. Eric doesn't enjoy team sports. _____, his brother Kyle plays basketball, baseball, and roller hockey.

active (adj.)   **as a result**   **practice** (v.)   **regularly** (adv.)

4. Many adults exercise _____. For example, some people run every morning before work.

5. Many children don't exercise every day. _____, some children are overweight.

6. Joseph is a very _____ child. He exercises all the time and plays many kinds of sports.

7. If you want to be a good swimmer, you must _____. You must swim several times a week.

therefore   condition (n.)   **likely** (adj.)

8. Some children are overweight. This _____ is sometimes a result of a poor diet.

9. Lynn's doctor told her to lose weight. _____, she is trying to eat less and exercise more.

10. Children who exercise are very _____ to grow up and continue to exercise as adults.

• D. Follow-up Activities

1. Refer to all the physical activities you and your classmates listed at the beginning of this chapter. Put these activities into the appropriate categories of **sports**, **exercise**, and **martial arts** in the chart below. Some activities may belong in more than one category. For example, swimming can be a sport or an exercise.

Martial Arts	Sports	Exercises
	swimming	swimming

2. Imagine that a friend has asked you to give suggestions for activities that children can do in order to get exercise. Work with two or three classmates. Make a list of ten ways that children can get exercise that would be fun for them. When you are finished, write your suggestions on the blackboard. As a class, decide which ten activities children will enjoy the most.

• E. Topics for Discussion and Writing

1. Refer back to the second follow-up activity. Write a letter to your friend and describe your ten recommendations.

2. Write in your journal. Describe the most exciting sports event you have ever watched or participated in. What was the event? What happened? Why was it exciting for you?

• F. Crossword Puzzle

Across

1. Joseph _____ roller hockey games on Sunday mornings.
2. Joseph is physically active, _____ many children are not.
3. Soccer, basketball, and baseball are _____.
5. Soccer and baseball _____ outdoor sports.
7. Children _____ exercise to be healthy.
8. Some children have a poor _____. This means that they do not eat healthy food.
10. Exercise can be _____. It can be enjoyable.
12. When children sit too much, they do not get enough _____ activity.
15. Joseph needs to exercise all his _____, not just while he is a child.
17. A team needs to _____ every week.
18. Joseph is a very _____ boy. He plays on many teams after school.
19. Some children are very _____ with sports. They play after school and on weekends, too.

Down

1. Regular exercise and a healthy diet are good _____ that we need all our lives.
3. **He, _____, it**
4. A person who is heavy, or fat, is _____.
6. Everyone needs to exercise _____. We need to exercise every week.
9. Children can do all kinds of _____, for example, running, jumping, or climbing rope.
11. Some conditions, such as being overweight, can be _____.
13. Joseph exercises every day. In _____, some children do not exercise at all.
14. Physical _____ means being in good physical condition.
16. We can do some sports alone, for example, running. We do other sports with a _____.

• G. Cloze Quiz

Read the following paragraphs. Fill in each space with the correct word from the list. Use each word only once.

busy	every	practices	winter
easy	morning	week	

   Joseph is a very (1)_____ 8-year-old boy. In the fall, he plays on a roller hockey team. He (2)_____ every Tuesday and Thursday afternoon and has a roller hockey game every Sunday (3)_____ . In the (4)_____ , Joseph plays basketball. His team has a basketball game (5)_____ Saturday morning. In the spring and summer, Joseph plays baseball. His team has a game twice a (6)_____ and practices often. It is (7)_____ to see that Joseph is very active after school.

active	exercise	result	trouble
believe	overweight	therefore	unhealthy

   Not all American children are as (8)_____ in sports after school as Joseph is. (9)_____ , these boys and girls need to (10)_____ in school. Many people believe that the fitness and health of American children are in (11)_____. In fact, forty percent of children age 5 to 8 may be (12)_____ already. For example, many have high blood pressure, are (13)_____, or have high cholesterol. Doctors (14)_____ that these conditions are the (15) _____ of physical inactivity and poor diet.

The New York City Marathon: A World Race

• Prereading Preparation

1. Look at the photograph on the left. How many people do you think are running in this marathon?

2. Read the title of this chapter. Why is the New York City Marathon a world race? Where is this race? Who runs in this race?

3. Work with two or three classmates. What are some reasons why people run in marathons? Make a list. Compare your list with your classmates' lists.

Directions: Read each paragraph carefully. Then answer the questions.

The New York City Marathon: A World Race

The New York City Marathon was started by a man named Fred Lebow. It began in 1970 as a small, unimportant race. Only 127 people ran, and just 55 of them finished. They ran around Central Park four times. Few people watched them run. However, over the years the marathon grew and became more popular.

Today people come from all over the world to run in the marathon. Runners must be at least 18 years old, but there is no age limit. In fact, the oldest runner was an 89-year-old man. Recently, more than 27,000 people ran in the New York City Marathon. Large crowds cheered the runners and offered the participants cold drinks and encouragement.

1. Only 127 people ran, and **just** 55 of them finished.

   Just means

   a. because
   b. only
   c. more than

2. _____ True _____ False   All 127 people finished the first marathon.

3. **Over the years** means

   a. as the years went by
   b. one year after
   c. many more years

4. _____ True _____ False   Runners cannot be younger than 18 years old.

5. **There is no age limit** means

   a. people of any age can run.
   b. older people cannot run.
   c. anyone older than 18 years old can run.

The course of the marathon has changed, too. Instead of running around Central Park, the participants go through the five boroughs of New York City: Queens, Brooklyn, Manhattan, the Bronx, and Staten Island. The marathon begins at the base of the Verrazano Narrows Bridge in Staten Island. The runners go across the bridge into Brooklyn. Then they go up through Queens and into the Bronx. The marathon finishes in Central Park in Manhattan. The complete course is 26 miles, 385 yards, and takes the best runners less than 3 hours.

6. The **course** of the marathon has changed, too. In this sentence, **course** means

   a. direction
   b. class
   c. reason

7. The **participants** are

   a. the crowd
   b. the runners
   c. the organizers

8. _____ True _____ False   The fastest runners can finish the race in 3 hours or more.

Although it has changed since 1970, the New York City Marathon is always exciting. Through the years, many unusual events have happened during the marathon. For example, Pat Tuz and John Weilbaker got married a few minutes before the race. Then, they ran the race with their wedding party. Some people run the whole marathon as a family. Other people run the race backwards.

In the fall of 1992, Fred Lebow, the founder of the New York City Marathon, slowly ran his last race. He was very ill with cancer, but he did not want to stop running. In October 1994, Fred died. However, the New York City Marathon, and all its excitement, will continue for many years to come.

9. _____ True _____ False   Pat Tuz and John Weilbaker ran the marathon backwards.

10. _____ True _____ False   Fred Lebow ran his last race in 1994.

11. **In the fall** means

   a. when someone fell down
   b. the time before winter
   c. the beginning of the year

NEW YORK CITY MARATHON ROUTE
(TOTAL DISTANCE 26.2 MILES)

Directions: Now read the complete passage. When you are finished, you will answer the questions that follow.

The New York City Marathon: A World Race

1   The New York City Marathon was started by a man named Fred
2 Lebow. It began in 1970 as a small, unimportant race. Only 127
3 people ran, and just 55 of them finished. They ran around Central
4 Park four times. Few people watched them run. However, over the
5 years the marathon grew and became more popular.
6   Today people come from all over the world to run in the
7 marathon. Runners must be at least 18 years old, but there is no
8 age limit. In fact, the oldest runner was an 89-year-old man.
9 Recently, more than 27,000 people ran in the New York City Marathon.
10 Large crowds cheered the runners and offered the participants
11 cold drinks and encouragement.
12   The course of the marathon has changed, too. Instead of
13 running around Central Park, the participants go through the five
14 boroughs of New York City: Queens, Brooklyn, Manhattan, the
15 Bronx, and Staten Island. The marathon begins at the base of the
16 Verrazano Narrows Bridge in Staten Island. The runners go across
17 the bridge into Brooklyn. Then they go up through Queens and
18 into the Bronx. The marathon finishes in Central Park in Manhattan.
19 The complete course is 26 miles, 385 yards, and takes the
20 best runners less than 3 hours.
21   Although it has changed since 1970, the New York City
22 Marathon is always exciting. Through the years, many unusual
23 events have happened during the marathon. For example, Pat Tuz and
24 John Weilbaker got married a few minutes before the race. Then
25 they ran the race with their wedding party. Some people run the
26 whole marathon as a family. Other people run the race backwards.
27   In the fall of 1992, Fred Lebow, the founder of the New York
28 City Marathon, slowly ran his last race. He was very ill with
29 cancer, but he did not want to stop running. In October 1994,
30 Fred died. However, the New York City Marathon, and all its
31 excitement, will continue for many years to come.

• A. Scanning for Information

Read the following questions. Then go back to the complete passage and scan quickly for the answers. Write them in the space under each question.

1. Describe two ways that the New York City Marathon has changed.

   a. _____

   b. _____

2. What do the crowds do during the marathon?

   _____

   _____

3. What are some unusual events that have happened during the marathon?

   _____

   _____

4. What is the main idea of this passage?
   a. The New York City Marathon began in 1970.
   b. The founder of the New York City Marathon was an important man.
   c. The New York City Marathon is a very popular and exciting race.

• B. Word Forms

In English, some verbs can become nouns when you add -*ment*, for example *agree* (v.), *agreement* (n.).

Read the following sentences. Decide if the correct word is a noun or a verb. Circle your answer. Do the example before you begin.

Example: a. My wife and I <u>agree/agreement</u> that we must both
                (v.)   (n.)

        take care of our children.

      b. This <u>agree/agreement</u> is very important to us.
         (v.)   (n.)

1. The crowds <u>excite/excitement</u> the runners in the marathon.
         (v.)   (n.)

2. There is a lot of <u>excite/excitement</u> all day.
           (v.)   (n.)

3. Many people <u>encourage/encouragement</u> the runners by
           (v.)   (n.)
cheering for them.

4. The crowds' <u>encourage/encouragement</u> is very important
          (v.)   (n.)
to the runners.

5. Andy has made a lot of <u>improve /improvement</u> in his English
          (v.)   (n.)
this semester.

6. Every day Andy's English <u>improves/improvement</u> a little more.
           (v.)   (n.)

7. English is a <u>require/requirement</u> in all American universities.
        <u>(v.)</u>   <u>(n.)</u>

8. All American universities also <u>require/requirement</u> a high
           (v.)   (n.)
school degree for all students.

• C. Vocabulary in Context

Read the following sentences. Choose the correct answer for each sentence. Write your answer in the blank space.

cheer (v.)   **encouragement** (n.)   **instead of**

1. The crowds _____ when they watch baseball games.

2. I want to go swimming, but it is raining. _____ going to the beach, I will go to the swimming pool at the college.

3. My parents always believed I could suceed. Their _____ helped me to do well in school.

course (n.)   **just** (adv.)   **limit** (n.)   **popular** (adj.)

4. Marathons are very _____ in American cities.

5. The speed _____ on this highway is 55 miles an hour. You cannot drive faster than 55.

6. The _____ for horse races is usually dirt, but sometimes it is grass.

7. I am taking _____ one class this semester because I have a job. I don't have time to take more than one class.

however   **participant** (n.)   **unusual** (adj.)

8. Snow is _____ in New York City in April. It very rarely happens.

9. Robert wants to be a _____in the next New York City Marathon. He runs 25 miles every week to prepare himself.

10. It is usually very cold in January. _____, this year it was very mild.

• D. Follow-up Activities

1. The following chart shows the number of participants in the
New York City Marathon from 1970 through 1994. Look at it
carefully, and then answer the questions that follow.

NEW YORK CITY MARATHON - WINNING TIMES

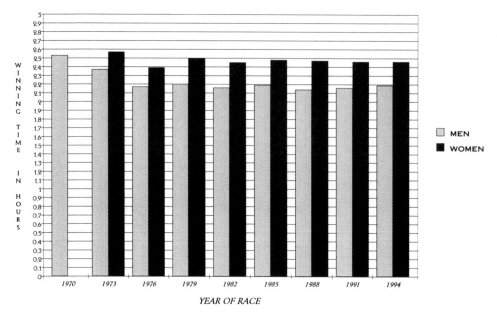

a. More than 3,000 people ran in the New York City Marathon
in 1976.

   1. Yes
   2. No

b. More than 18,000 people ran in the New York City Marathon
in 1985.

   1. Yes
   2. No

c. More than 27,000 people ran in the New York City Marathon
in 1991.

   1. Yes
   2. No

d. More than 27,000 people ran in the New York City Marathon
in 1994.
   1. Yes
   2. No

e. The largest increase in the number of runners occurred from 1976 to 1979.

   1. Yes
   2. No

2. The following chart shows the finishing times of the men and women participants in the New York City Marathon from 1970 through 1994. Look at it carefully. Then read the sentences that follow. Fill in the blank with the word **women** or **men** to make the sentence correct.

NEW YORK CITY MARATHON - NUMBER OF RUNNERS

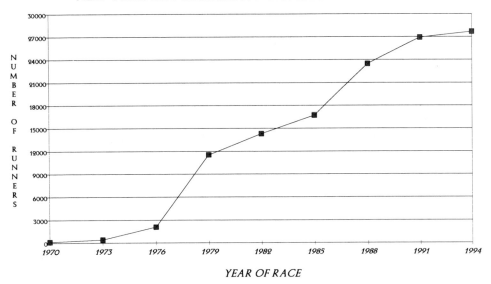

YEAR OF RACE

Look at the chart above.

   a. In 1970 only _____ ran in the Marathon.

   b. In 1985 the winning time for _____ was 2.2 hours.

   c. In 1979 the winning time for _____ was 2.5 hours.

   d. In 1994 the winning time for _____ was 2.2 hours.

• E. Topics for Discussion and Writing

1. Work with two or three classmates. Have you or your partners ever run in a marathon? How did you prepare for it? What was the race like? If you haven't run in a marathon, do you want to? Why or why not?

2. Imagine that your friend wants to run in a marathon. In your group, discuss some advice that you can give your friend. Compare your suggestions with your other classmates' suggestions. Which suggestions are the best? Write a letter to your friend and give him or her your advice.

3. Write in your journal. Describe a popular sports event in your country. What is the event? Who participates? Why do people enjoy watching it?

• F. Crossword Puzzle

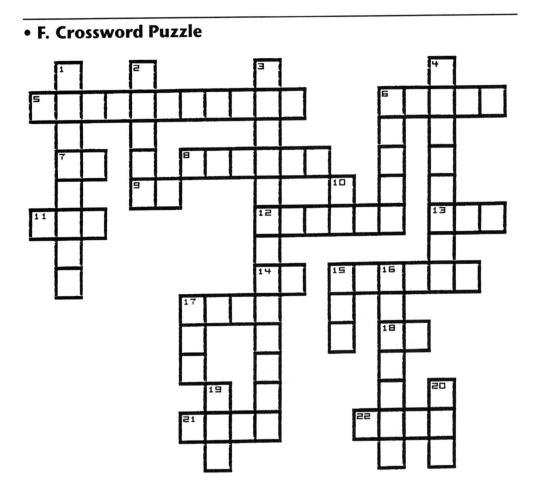

Across

5. Each _____ in the race gets a number for identification.
6. A huge _____ of people lines the route of the race in order to watch.
7. The race begins _____ the base of the Verrazano Narrows Bridge.
8. Everyone runs _____ the bridge from Staten Island to Brooklyn.
9. Many people want _____ run in the New York City race.
11. he, _____, it
12. Every _____ has trained for many months.
13. At the end of the race, all the athletes _____ a medal.
14. People from all over the world _____ to New York to be in the race.
15. The _____ of the race runs through all the boroughs of New York City.
17. The _____ is about 26 miles in length.
18. I, me; we, _____.
21. In the first race, _____ half the people finished.
22. The race is always held in the _____, when the weather is cool.

Down

1. A _____ is a 26-mile race.
2. There is no age _____ for the race. Some very old people have run in this race.
3. The people who watch the race offer _____ to the runners.
4. Brooklyn, Queens, Manhattan, Staten Island, and the Bronx are the five _____ of New York City.
6. The people who watch the race _____ as the runners pass them on the route.
10. The race is always held _____ Sunday.
15. Thousands of people run in the race, but not everyone _____ finish it.
16. Sometimes people do _____, or strange, things during the race.
17. Most people _____ in the race, but some people simply walk fast.
19. Only a few people win the race, _____ everyone feels successful.
20. each; every

• G. Cloze Quiz

Read the following paragraphs. Fill in each space with the correct word from the list. Use each word only once.

cheered	limit	oldest	recently
encouragement	marathon	participants	

Today people come from all over the world to run in the
(1) _____. Runners must be at least 18 years old, but
there is no age (2)_____ . In fact, the (3)_____
runner was an 89-year-old man. (4)_____ , more than
27,000 people ran in the New York City Marathon. Large crowds
(5)_____ the runners and offered the (6) _____
cold drinks and (7)_____ .

backwards	example	race	since
events	exciting	ran	whole

Although it has changed (8) _____1970, the New York
City Marathon is always (9)_____ . Through the years,
many unusual (10) _____ have happened during the
marathon. For (11) _____, Pat Tuz and John Weilbaker
got married a few minutes before the (12) _____.
Then they (13) _____the race with their wedding party.
Some people run the (14) _____ marathon as a family.
Other people run the race (15)_____ .

Remarkable Researchers

Margaret Mead:
The World Was Her Home

Work with a classmate to discuss these questions.

1. Look at the photograph on the opposite page. The woman on the left was Margaret Mead. She was American.

   a. What was her occupation? What do you think?

      1. She was an artist.
      2. She was an anthropologist.
      3. She was a doctor.

   b. What kind of work did Margaret Mead do?

      1. She helped sick people.
      2. She painted pictures.
      3. She studied different cultures.

   c. Where did Margaret Mead do most of her work?

      1. in her own country
      2. in a hospital
      3. in different countries

2. Describe the kind of work that you think Margaret Mead did. Write one or two sentences.

   _____

   _____

   _____

3. Read the title of this chapter. Why do you think the whole world was Margaret Mead's home? How can the world be a person's home?

Directions: Read each paragraph carefully. Then answer the questions.

Margaret Mead: The World Was Her Home

Margaret Mead was a famous American anthropologist. She was born on December 16, 1901, in Philadelphia, Pennsylvania. She lived with her parents, her grandmother, and her brother and sisters. Her parents were both teachers, and her grandmother was a teacher, too. They believed that education was very important for children. They believed that the world was important, too. Margaret learned many things from her parents and grandmother.

When she was a child, Margaret's family traveled often and lived in many different towns. Margaret was always interested in people and places, so she decided to study anthropology in college to learn about different cultures. At that time it was not very common for women to study in a university. It was even more unusual for women to study anthropology.

1. _____ True _____ False   Margaret Mead's parents were anthropologists.

2. What do these two paragraphs discuss?

    a. Margaret's education as a young child
    b. the importance of Margaret's family and childhood
    c. the importance of Margaret's occupation

3. Why did Margaret decide to study anthropology?

_____

4. What do you think the next part of the passage will discuss?

_____

Margaret graduated from college in 1923. She wanted to continue her education in anthropology, so she decided to go to American Samoa to study about young women there. Many people did not know about the culture of American Samoa. Margaret wanted to learn about Samoans so that the world could learn about them, too.

Margaret lived in Samoa for nine months and learned the language. She talked with the Samoan people, especially the teenage girls. She ate with them, danced with them, and learned many details about their peaceful culture.

5. _____ True _____ False   Margaret went to Samoa to continue her education in anthropology.

6. Why did Margaret want to learn about the Samoan culture?

    a. She wanted to go to college in Samoa.
    b. She wanted to teach the world about Samoa.
    c. She wanted to learn the Samoan language.

7. How long did Margaret live in Samoa? _____

8. _____ True _____ False   Margaret knew the Samoan language before she went to Samoa.

9. She talked with the Samoan people, **especially** the **teenage girls**.

    a. **Especially** means

        1. only
        2. most importantly
        3. except for

    b. **Teenage girls** are

        1. girls from 13 to 19 years old
        2. girls from 7 to 14 years old
        3. girls over 18 years old

10. _____ True _____ False   The Samoan culture was peaceful.

When Margaret returned to the United States, she wrote a book about the young Samoan women she studied. The book was called *Coming of Age in Samoa*, and it was very popular. As a result, Margaret Mead became very famous. Before Margaret wrote her book, not many people were interested in anthropology. Because of Margaret's book, anthropology became a popular subject.

Margaret Mead studied many different cultures in her life. She continued to work, travel, write, and teach until she died in 1978. She was a remarkable woman of the world.

11. ***Coming of Age in Samoa*** was

    a. a book
    b. a magazine
    c. a teenage girl

12. What was the subject of Margaret's book?

    _____

13. Why did Margaret Mead become famous?

    a. because she was an anthropologist
    b. because she studied many cultures
    c. because she wrote a popular book

14. Margaret Mead continued to work, travel, write, and teach **until** she died in 1978.

    a. **Until** means

        1. when something begins
        2. when something continues
        3. when something stops

    b. Complete the following sentence.
       Last night Elizabeth studied at the library until

        1. it opened
        2. it closed
        3. she woke up

15. Margaret Mead was a **remarkable** woman of the world.

    Remarkable means

        a. educated
        b. hard-working
        c. unusual

Directions: Read the complete passage. When you are finished, answer the questions that follow.

Margaret Mead: The World Was Her Home

1   Margaret Mead was a famous American anthropologist. She was
2 born on December 16, 1901, in Philadelphia, Pennsylvania. She
3 lived with her parents, her grandmother, and her brother and sis-
4 ters. Her parents were both teachers, and her grandmother was a
5 teacher, too. They believed that education was very important for
6 children. They believed that the world was important, too. Margaret
7 learned many things from her parents and grandmother.
8   When she was a child, Margaret's family traveled often and lived
9 in many different towns. Margaret was always interested in people
10 and places, so she decided to study anthropology in college to learn
11 about different cultures. At that time it was not very common for
12 women to study in a university. It was even more unusual for
13 women to study anthropology.
14   Margaret graduated from college in 1923. She wanted to con-
15 tinue her education in anthropology, so she decided to go to Ameri-
16 can Samoa to study about young women there. Many people did not
17 know about the culture of American Samoa. Margaret wanted to
18 learn about Samoans so that the world could learn about them, too.
19   Margaret lived in Samoa for nine months and learned the lan-
20 guage. She talked with the Samoan people, especially the teenage
21 girls. She ate with them, danced with them, and learned many de-
22 tails about their peaceful culture.

23   When Margaret returned to the United States, she wrote a book
24 about the young Samoan women she studied. The book was called
25 *Coming of Age in Samoa*, and it was very popular. As a result, Mar-
26 garet Mead became very famous. Before Margaret wrote her book,
27 not many people were interested in anthropology. Because of
28 Margaret's book, anthropology became a popular subject.
29   Margaret Mead studied many different cultures in her life. She
30 continued to work, travel, write, and teach until she died in 1978.
31 She was a remarkable woman of the world.

• A. Scanning for Information

Read the following questions. Then go back to the complete passage
and scan quickly for the answers. Write them in the space under each
question.

1. Margaret Mead decided to study anthropology in college to
   learn about different cultures.

   a. Why do you think she made this decision?

   _____

   _____

   b. Was this an unusual decision? Why or why not?

   _____

   _____

2. How did Margaret study the Samoan people?

   _____

   _____

3. What did Margaret Mead contribute to anthropology? In other
   words, why was Margaret Mead important to anthropology?

   _____

4. What is the main idea of this passage?

   _____

   _____

• B. Word Forms

In English, some verbs (v.) become nouns (n.) by adding the suffix *-ence* or *-ance* to the verb. Read the following sentences. Decide if the correct word is a noun or a verb. Circle your answer.

1. Children <u>depend / dependence</u> on their parents for everything.
        (v.)   (n.)

2. This <u>depend / dependence</u> usually continues until they
      (v.)   (n.)

   complete high school.

3. Eric's <u>appears / appearance</u> changed in many ways as he
      (v.)   (n.)
   became older.

4. For example, he <u>appears / appearance</u> thinner, and his hair
        (v.)   (n.)
   is turning gray.

5. My sister and I <u>differ / difference</u> from each other in many ways.
       (v.)   (n.)

6. Because of our <u>differ / differences</u>, we are not very close.
       (v.)   (n.)

7. Sharks prefer warm water. They <u>avoid / avoidance</u> cold water.
          (v.)   (n.)

8. Their <u>avoid / avoidance</u> of cold water helps them to survive.
      (v.)   (n.)

• C. Vocabulary in Context

Read the following sentences. Choose the correct answer for each sentence. Write your answer in the blank space. Use each word only once.

especially (adv.)   **remarkable** (adj.)   **believe** (v.)

1. Helen enjoys all her classes, but she _____ likes her English class. That is her favorite subject.

2. My brother and I exercise every day. We _____ that exercise is important for good health.

3. Sharks are _____ animals. They hunt for food at night by feeling vibrations in the water.

cultures (n.)   **peaceful** (adj.)   **as a result**

4. The Samoans are very _____ people. They rarely disagree or fight with each other.

5. Choi and Marina come from different _____, but they are very good friends.

6. Maria did not do her homework last night. _____, she was not prepared for class today.

until (prep.) **interested** (adj.) **details** (n.) **popular** (adj.)

7. That is a very _____ type of car. Many people buy it because it is inexpensive and reliable.

8. Cesar is _____ in medicine. He wants to become a doctor.

9. I studied last night _____ midnight. Then I went to sleep.

10. There was an earthquake in California this morning, but I don't know the _____. I want to listen to the radio to learn more about it.

• D. Follow-up Activities

1. Refer back to the Prereading section. Read your description of the work that you thought Margaret Mead did. How accurate was your description?

2. Work with two or three partners. Imagine that you are a team of anthropologists. You are going to a different country to study a different culture. You plan to interview the people there to learn about their culture. What special features of this culture do you want to learn most about? What questions can you ask to get this information? Together, make a list of questions for your interview. When you are finished, write your questions on the blackboard. Discuss all the groups' questions and, as a class, make up one questionnaire.

3. Use your questionnaire to interview someone from a culture that is different from your own. You may interview someone in your class, but a person outside your class would be better. Bring the answers back to class. Discuss what you learned from your interview about this person's culture.

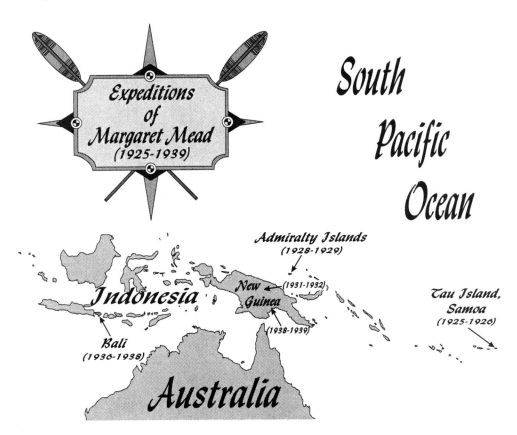

• E. Topics for Discussion and Writing

1. Describe one or two interesting things you have learned about American culture. Write a paragraph. How did you learn these things about American culture?

2. Describe someone important in your culture. This may be someone who is alive now or who lived in the past. Write a paragraph about this person. When you are finished, give your description to a classmate and read your classmate's description of an important person in his or her culture. Then discuss what you learned about your classmate's culture by reading about this person.

3. Do you think anthropology is important? Why or why not? Write a paragraph to explain your opinion. Give some examples.

4. Write in your journal. Imagine that you are a student of anthropology. Decide what culture you want to study. Discuss your reasons in a paragraph.

• F. Crossword Puzzle

Across
1. Margaret Mead went to _____ at a time when it was not common for women to go to a university.
4. Margaret Mead was a very _____ person. Many people knew her and read her books.
7. Margaret Mead was an _____.
12. Margaret Mead studied different people and their _____.
13. Because of Margaret Mead, many people became very _____ in learning about other cultures.
14. American _____ was the first country Margaret Mead went to and studied.
15. Margaret Mead studied many _____ about people's lives, such as what they ate.
16. Margaret Mead learned to _____ other languages.

Down
2. Margaret Mead was interested in other people, _____ young women and their lives.
3. Margaret Mead traveled all over the _____.
5. Margaret Mead wrote many _____ about the cultures she studied.
6. Margaret Mead's first book made her _____.
8. It is _____ for everyone to understand other people's cultures.
9. Today it is not _____ for women to go to a university to study anthropology.
10. Because of all she did in her life, Margaret Mead was a very _____ woman.
11. The first culture that Margaret Mead studied was very _____. These people were very gentle.

• G. Cloze Quiz

Read the passage below. Fill in each space with the correct word from the list. Use each word only once.

about	decided	graduated	study
culture	education	learn	

Margaret (1) _____ from college in 1923. She wanted to continue her (2)_____ in anthropology, so she (3)_____ to go to American Samoa to (4)_____ the young women there. Many people did not know about the (5)_____ of American Samoa. Margaret wanted to learn (6)_____ Samoans so that the world could (7)_____ about them, too.

because	interested	result	subject
book	popular	returned	wrote

When Margaret (8)_____ to the United States from Samoa, she (9)_____ a book about the young Samoan women she studied. The (10)_____ was called *Coming of Age in Samoa*, and it was very (11)_____ . As a (12)_____ , Margaret Mead became very famous. Before Margaret wrote her book, not many people were (13)_____ in anthropology. (14)_____ of Margaret's book, anthropology became a popular (15)_____ , and many people began to read about different cultures.

Louis Pasteur:
A Modern-Day Scientist

• Prereading Preparation

Work with a classmate to discuss these questions.

1. Look at the photograph on the left. This man was Louis Pasteur.

   a. What kind of scientific work did he do? What do you think?

      1. He was an inventor.
      2. He was a chemist.
      3. He was a medical doctor.

   b. Where did Louis Pasteur do his work?

      1. in a laboratory
      2. in a hospital
      3. in an office

2. Read the title of this chapter.

   a. How is modern scientific work different from scientific work that people did hundreds of years ago?
   b. Why do you think Louis Pasteur was a modern-day scientist?

Directions: Read each paragraph carefully. Then answer the questions.

Louis Pasteur: A Modern-Day Scientist

In the summer of 1885, nine-year-old Joseph Meister was a very ill little boy. He had been attacked by a sick dog that had rabies, a deadly disease. His doctor tried to help him, but there was no cure for rabies at that time. The doctor told Joseph's parents that perhaps there was one man who could save Joseph's life. His name was Louis Pasteur.

1. A **disease** is

   a. a summer activity
   b. an attack by an animal
   c. an illness; a sickness

2. What is rabies?

   _____

3. Did Joseph have rabies?

   a. Yes
   b. No

4. a. Was Joseph's doctor able to help him? _____

   b. Why or why not?

   _____

5. A **cure** for a disease is

   a. a medicine or treatment that makes an illness go away
   b. a careful description of that disease in a book
   c. a special doctor who knows about that disease

6. **His name was Louis Pasteur.** Who does this refer to?

   a. Joseph's parents
   b. Joseph's doctor
   c. the man who could save Joseph's life

7. What do you think the next paragraph will discuss?

   a. Joseph's life after he became well again
   b. the life of Joseph's doctor
   c. Louis Pasteur's life

When Pasteur was a young boy in France, he was very curious. Louis was especially interested in medicine, so he spent many hours every day with the chemist who lived in his small town. The chemist sold pills, cough syrups, and other types of medicine, just as modern pharmacists, or druggists, do today. At that time, the chemist had to make all the medicines himself. Young Louis enjoyed watching the chemist as he worked and listening to him assist the customers who came to him each day. Pasteur decided that one day he wanted to help people, too.

As a schoolboy, Pasteur worked slowly and carefully. At first, his teachers thought that young Louis might be a slow learner. Through elementary school, high school, and college, Pasteur worked the same thoughtful way. In fact, he was not a slow learner, but a very intelligent young man. He became a college professor and a scientist, and he continued to work very carefully.

8. Louis was **especially** interested in medicine, **so** he spent many hours every day with the chemist who lived in his small town.

   a. **Especially** means

      1. mostly
      2. probably
      3. originally

   b. **So** means

      1. because
      2. as a result
      3. all the time

9. Louis was a very **curious** person. He enjoyed watching the chemist as he worked and listening to the chemist **assist** his customers.

   a. **Curious** means

      1. very hard-working
      2. very careful
      3. very interested in learning

   b. **Assist** means

      1. help
      2. sell
      3. work

10. Why did Louis spend many hours with the chemist?

   a. Louis was interested in medicine.
   b. Louis wanted to become a chemist.
   c. The chemist needed Louis' help.

11. The chemist sold pills, cough syrups, and other types of medicine, **just as pharmacists,** or druggists, **do today**.

   a. **Just as** means

     1. only
     2. the same as
     3. whereas

   b. **Pharmacists** are _____ .

   c. What do pharmacists **do today?**

   _____

12. **As a schoolboy**, Pasteur worked slowly and carefully. **At first**, his teachers thought that young Louis might be a slow learner.

   a. **As a schoolboy** means

     1. Louis acted like a little boy
     2. when Louis was a boy in school
     3. boys in school always work slowly

   b. **At first** means

     1. in the beginning
     2. one time
     3. for one reason

   c. Why did his teacher think Louis might be a slow learner?

   _____

13. _____ True _____ False   Louis was a slow learner and not an intelligent man.

14. _____ True _____ False   Louis continued to work very carefully when he became a professor and a scientist.

15. What do you think the next part of the passage will discuss?

_____

Because of Pasteur's patient methods, he was able to make many observations about germs. For example, germs cause meat and milk to spoil. They also cause many serious diseases. Pasteur was studying about the germs that cause rabies when Joseph Meister became ill. In fact, Pasteur believed he had a cure for rabies, but he had never given it to a person before. At first, Pasteur was afraid to treat Joseph, but his doctor said the child was dying. Pasteur gave Joseph an inoculation, or shot, every day for ten days. Slowly, the child became better. Pasteur's vaccination cured him.

16. Why was Pasteur able to make many observations about germs?

    a. because he was very intelligent
    b. because he was patient
    c. because germs cause food to spoil

17. Germs cause meat and milk to **spoil**. Spoil means

    a. become warm
    b. become uneatable
    c. become cold

18. Why was Pasteur afraid to treat Joseph at first?

    a. He had never given the cure to a human before.
    b. He did not think he could cure rabies.
    c. His doctor said the child was dying.

19. a. What is an **inoculation**?

    _____

    b. **Every day for ten days** is

       1. ten shots every day
       2. one shot after ten days
       3. one shot each day for ten days

20. Why did the child become better?

    _____

    _____

During his lifetime, Pasteur studied germs and learned how they cause diseases in animals and people. He developed vaccinations that prevent many of these illnesses. He also devised the process of pasteurization, which stops foods such as milk from spoiling. Louis Pasteur died on September 28, 1895, at the age of 72. Modern medicine continues to benefit from the work of this great scientist.

21. **During his lifetime** means

    a. in the years that he lived
    b. after he became a college professor
    c. when Joseph Meister was ill

22. **Prevent** means

    a. describe something carefully
    b. help something happen
    c. stop something from happening

23. What can **vaccinations** do?

    a. help keep animals and people healthy
    b. cause illnesses
    c. stop food from spoiling

24. Pasteur **devised** the **process** of pasteurization.

    a. **Devised** means
       1. named
       2. invented
       3. liked

    b. A **process** is a
       1. medical treatment
       2. way to make money
       3. specific way of doing something

    c. **The process of pasteurization**
       1. prevents disease
       2. causes illnesses
       3. prevents milk from spoiling

25. **Modern medicine** continues to **benefit** from the work of this great scientist.

    a. **Modern medicine** means

        1. medicine in the past
        2. medicine today
        3. vaccinations

    b. When we **benefit** from something, we

        1. get an advantage
        2. get a disadvantage

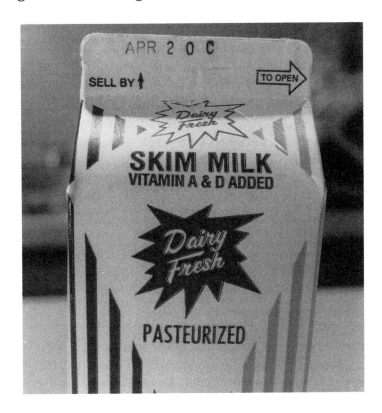

Directions: Read the complete passage. When you are finished, you will answer the questions that follow.

Louis Pasteur: A Modern-Day Scientist

1   In the summer of 1885, nine-year-old Joseph Meister was a very
2 ill little boy. He had been attacked by a sick dog that had rabies, a
3 deadly disease. His doctor tried to help him, but there was no cure
4 for rabies at that time. The doctor told Joseph's parents that per-
5 haps there was one man who could save Joseph's life. His name was
6 Louis Pasteur.
7   When Pasteur was a young boy in France, he was very curious.
8 Louis was especially interested in medicine, so he spent many
9 hours every day with the chemist who lived in his small town. The
10 chemist sold pills, cough syrups, and other types of medicine, just
11 as modern pharmacists, or druggists, do today. At that time, the
12 chemist had to make all the medicines himself. Young Louis en-
13 joyed watching the chemist as he worked and listening to him as-
14 sist the customers who came to him each day. Pasteur decided that
15 one day he wanted to help people, too.
16   As a schoolboy, Pasteur worked slowly and carefully. At first, his
17 teachers thought that young Louis might be a slow learner. Through
18 elementary school, high school, and college, Pasteur worked the
19 same thoughtful way. In fact, he was not a slow learner, but a very
20 intelligent young man. He became a college professor and a scien-
21 tist, and he continued to work very carefully.
22   Because of Pasteur's patient methods, he was able to make many
23 observations about germs. For example, germs cause meat and milk
24 to spoil. They also cause many serious diseases. Pasteur was study-
25 ing about the germs that cause rabies when Joseph Meister became
26 ill. In fact, Pasteur believed he had a cure for rabies, but he had
27 never given it to a person before. At first, Pasteur was afraid to
28 treat Joseph, but his doctor said the child was dying. Pasteur gave
29 Joseph an inoculation, or shot, every day for ten days. Slowly, the
30 child became better. Pasteur's vaccination cured him.
31   During his lifetime, Pasteur studied germs and learned how they
32 cause diseases in animals and people. He developed vaccinations
33 that prevent many of these illnesses. He also devised the process of
34 pasteurization, which stops foods such as milk from spoiling. Louis
35 Pasteur died on September 28, 1895, at the age of 72. Modern medi-
36 cine continues to benefit from the work of this great scientist.

• A. Scanning for Information

Read the following questions. Then go back to the complete passage and scan quickly for the answers. Write them in the space under each question.

1. Why did Pasteur decide he wanted to help people?

   _____

   _____

2. Why did Pasteur agree to treat Joseph?

   _____

   _____

3. What were some of Pasteur's observations about germs?

   a. _____

   b. _____

4. What is the main idea of this passage?

   a. Louis Pasteur saved Joseph Meister's life by developing a cure for rabies.
   b. Louis Pasteur was a great scientist whose work continues to help science today.
   c. Louis Pasteur learned about germs and developed the process of pasteurization.

• B. Word Forms

In English, some verbs (v.) become nouns (n.) by dropping the final -
e and adding the suffix -*tion*, for example, *graduate* (v.), *graduation*
(n.). Read the following sentences. Does each sentence need a noun
or a verb? Circle the correct answer.

1. Sociologists frequently observe / observation people in public
                               (v.)   (n.)

   places such as stores and parks.

2. Sociologists record their observe / observations in journals.
                                    (v.)   (n.)

3. Claire's educates / education included music lessons.
              (v.)   (n.)

4. Claire's parents educated / education her to become a concert
                           (v.)   (n.)
   violinist.

5. In the United States, children need to have certain
   vaccinates / vaccinations before they may begin school.
        (v.)   (n.)

6. In the United States, doctors vaccinate / vaccination children
                              (v.)   (n.)

   for several serious diseases.

7. Paige continued / continuation to study after she graduated
          (v.)   (n.)

   college.

8. Paige believed that the continued / continuation of her
                             (v.)   (n.)

   education was very important.

• C. Vocabulary in Context

Read the following sentences. Choose the correct answer for each sentence. Write your answer in the blank space.

at first   because of   cure (n.)   **decided** (v.)

1. Don was very sick last year. _____ his long illness, he missed two months of school.

2. Maria didn't speak English when she came to the United States. _____ she didn't understand anyone, but gradually she learned to communicate very well.

3. Last year, Monica _____ to change her job because she wasn't happy with her work.

4. Doctors do not have a _____ for the common cold, but they do for many serious diseases.

assisted (v.) **careful** (adj.) **for example   process** (n.)

5. Alexandra is always very _____ when she walks across the street. She looks in both directions for cars.

6. Making paper is a simple _____.

7. Three nurses _____ the doctor during the child's medical treatment.

8. Modern pharmacies sell many different products in addition to medicine. _____, they sell magazines, candy, toys, and cards.

caused (v.)   **curious** (adj.)   **in fact**

9. Our college basketball team is very good. _____, the team lost only one game last year.

10. Cats are very _____ animals. They are interested in looking at everything.

11. Last winter, the ice on the roads _____ many car accidents.

• D. Follow-up Activities

1. Louis Pasteur's discovery of a rabies vaccine saved many lives.
    What other discoveries help to save lives today? Work in small
    groups with your classmates, and discuss your ideas. Then com-
    plete the chart below. When you are finished, compare your chart
    with your other classmates' charts. As a class, discuss these
    discoveries. Decide which discovery is the most important one.

Discoveries	Illnesses Cured
rabies vaccine	rabies

2. Pasteur developed the process of pasteurization 100 years ago
    to make milk safe to drink. Today we know many other ways to
    prevent food from spoiling. Work with one or two classmates.
    Talk about some of these ways. Make a list, and compare it with
    your other classmates' lists. Discuss which way is the most
    important, and why.

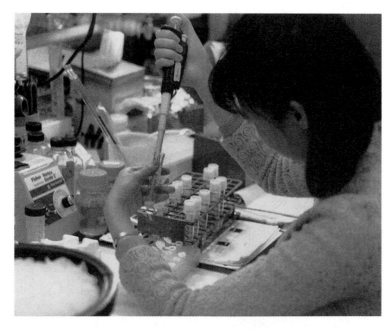

• E. Topics for Discussion and Writing

1. Look at the follow-up activity on page 122. Which discovery do you think is the most important? Write a paragraph. Tell why this discovery is important. Describe how it has helped people.

2. Many medical discoveries will be made in the future. What do you think will be the most important cure? Why? Discuss your ideas with your classmates. Decide which cures are the most important. Give your reasons.

3. Write in your journal. Think of a time when you or someone you know was not well. Describe the situation. What treatment helped this person? How did it help?

• F. Crossword Puzzle

Across

2. Pasteur worked slowly and carefully. He was a very _____ man.
3. Some illnesses kill people. These diseases are _____.
4. After class, the students _____ home.
5. Aspirin and cough syrup are types of _____.
9. At first, Pasteur did _____ want to inoculate Joseph Meister.
10. Germs cause milk to _____.
12. People who want to know all about many things are very _____.
16. Joseph Meister was dying, _____ Pasteur inoculated him, even though he was afraid.
17. Pasteur discovered the _____ for rabies. His vaccination saved many people from rabies.
18. ill; not well
19. We all _____ from medical discoveries.
20. The past of **eat**
21. There is a _____ for many types of diseases.
23. Pasteur did not live in a big city. He lived in a small _____.
25. Pasteur died _____ 1895.

Down

1. Many people _____ alive today because of Pasteur's vaccine.
2. A _____, or druggist, prepares medicine.
3. Pasteur _____ his work slowly and carefully.
4. _____ can cause disease.
6. People who shop in stores are called _____.
7. each; every
8. We protect ourselves against some diseases with an _____, or shot.
11. Pasteur was born _____ 1823.
12. We _____ buy medicine in a drugstore, or pharmacy.
13. _____ is a serious disease. We can get it from an animal bite.
14. Pasteur liked to _____, or help, the druggist.
15. Vaccinations help _____ many kinds of illnesses.
21. Vaccinations are _____ important for children.
22. Pasteur was a professor. He was a scientist, _____.
24. You and I

• G. Cloze Quiz

Read the following paragraphs. Fill in each space with the correct word from the list. Use each word only once.

became	carefully	school	thoughtful
but	learner	scientist	

As a schoolboy, Pasteur always worked slowly and (1)_____ . At first, his teachers thought that young Louis might be a slow (2)_____ . Through elementary school, high (3)_____ , and college, Pasteur worked the same (4)_____ way. In fact, he was not a slow learner, (5)_____ a very intelligent young man. He (6)_____ a college professor and a (7)_____ , and he continued to work very carefully.

age	devised	illnesses	studied
benefit	during	prevent	such

(8)_____ his lifetime, Pasteur (9)_____ germs, and learned how they cause (10)_____ in animals and people. He developed vaccinations that (11)_____ many diseases. He also (12)_____ the process of pasteurization, which stops foods (13)_____ as milk from spoiling. Louis Pasteur died on September 28, 1895, at the (14)_____ of 72. Modern medicine continues to (15)_____ from the work of this great scientist.

Science and History

The Origin of the Moon

---

1. What do you know about the moon? Work with your teacher and your classmates. Try to answer the following questions.

Questions	Answers
How far is the Earth from the moon?	
How old is the moon?	
Does the moon have an atmosphere?	
Where did the moon come from?	
Is there life on the moon?	

Directions: Read each paragraph carefully. Then answer the questions.

The Origins of the Moon

For thousands of years, people have looked up at the night sky and looked at the moon. They wondered what the moon was made of. They wanted to know how big it was and how far away it was. One of the most interesting questions was "Where did the moon come from?" No one knew for sure. Scientists developed many different theories, or guesses, but they could not prove that their ideas were correct.

Then, between 1969 and 1972, the United States sent astronauts to the moon. They studied the moon and returned to Earth with rock samples. Scientists have studied these pieces of rock, the moon's movements, and information about the moon and the Earth. They can finally answer questions about the origin of the moon.

1. **People wondered what the moon was made of.** When people looked at the moon, they felt

    a. curious
    b. afraid
    c. cold

2. _____True _____ False   Thousands of years ago, people knew how big the moon is.

3. _____True _____ False   Thousands of years ago, people knew how far away the moon is from the Earth.

4. Scientists developed many different **theories**, or guesses, but they could not prove that their ideas were correct.

    a. A **theory** is

        1. a correct idea
        2. something you already proved
        3. a guess

    b. Scientists had

        1. an idea that they were sure about
        2. an idea that they were not sure about

5. **Astronauts** are people who

    a. study rocks
    b. travel in space
    c. live on the moon

6. _____ True _____ False   Scientists think that they know the origin of the moon.

7. What do you think the next paragraph will discuss?

_____

Today most scientists believe that the moon formed from the Earth. They think that a large object hit the Earth early in its history. Perhaps the object was as big as Mars. When the object hit the Earth, huge pieces of the Earth broke off. These pieces went into orbit around the Earth. After a brief time, the pieces came together and formed the moon.

This "impact theory" explains many facts about the Earth and the moon. For example, the moon is very dry because the impact created so much heat that it dried up all the water. The Earth has iron in its center. However, the moon has very little iron in its center. This is because the moon formed from lighter materials that make up the outer part of the Earth. Finally, the Earth and the moon are almost the same age: the Earth is about 4.5 billion years old, and the moon is about 4.4 billion years old.

8. Scientists think that a large object hit the Earth **early in its history.** When the object hit the Earth,

    a. people saw it happen
    b. the Earth was new
    c. people wrote about it

9. An **orbit** is

    a. a path or route around something in space
    b. a large distance in space
    c. a large rock in space

10. An **impact** means

    a. an object moves past another object
    b. an object hits another object

11. Scientists believe that in the past,

    a. the moon was part of the Earth
    b. the moon was close to Mars
    c. the moon hit the Earth

12. Scientists believe that

    a. the moon was always in one piece
    b. the moon is made up of many big pieces

13. The astronauts brought back pieces of rock from the moon. It is probably true that

    a. the rock from the moon is just like rock on Earth
    b. the rock from the moon is different from rock on Earth

14. The "impact theory" describes

    a. scientists' belief about the size of the Earth and Mars
    b. scientists' belief about the origin of the moon

15. How many facts about the Earth and the moon are in this paragraph?

    a. two
    b. three
    c. four

16. Which statement is true?

    a. The Earth is 4.5 billion years old, and the moon is, too.
    b. The moon is 4.5 billion years old, but the Earth isn't.
    c. The Earth is 4.5 billion years old, but the moon isn't.

No one can prove that something really happened billions of years ago. In the future, new information will either support this theory or show that it is wrong. For now, scientists accept the impact theory because it explains what we know today about the Earth and the moon.

17. _____ True _____ False   Scientists are sure that their idea is correct.

18. **In the future, new information will either support this theory or show that it is wrong.** Information that supports the scientists' theory

    a. helps prove the theory is correct
    b. helps prove the theory is wrong

19. Scientists accept the impact theory because

    a. no one can prove that the impact theory isn't true
    b. the information they have about the Earth and the moon supports the impact theory

Directions: Read the complete passage. When you are finished, you will answer the questions that follow.

The Origin of the Moon

1   For thousands of years, people have looked up at the night sky
2   and looked at the moon. They wondered what the moon was made
3   of. They wanted to know how big it was and how far away it was.
4   One of the most interesting questions was "Where did the moon
5   come from?" No one knew for sure. Scientists developed many dif-
6   ferent theories, or guesses, but they could not prove that their
7   ideas were correct.
8   Then, between 1969 and 1972, the United States sent astronauts
9   to the moon. They studied the moon and returned to Earth with
10 rock samples. Scientists have studied these pieces of rock, the
11 moon's movements, and information about the moon and the Earth.
12 They can finally answer questions about the origin of the moon.
13   Today most scientists believe that the moon formed from the
14 Earth. They think that a large object hit the Earth early in its his-
15 tory. Perhaps the object was as big as Mars. When the object hit the
16 Earth, huge pieces of the Earth broke off. These pieces went into or-
17 bit around the Earth. After a brief time, the pieces came together
18 and formed the moon.
19   This "impact theory" explains many facts about the Earth and the
20 moon. For example, the moon is very dry because the impact cre-
21 ated so much heat that it dried up all the water. The Earth has iron
22 in its center. However, the moon has very little iron in its center.
23 This is because the moon formed from lighter materials that make
24 up the outer part of the Earth. Finally, the Earth and the moon are
25 almost the same age: the Earth is about 4.5 billion years old, and
26 the moon is about 4.4 billion years old.
27   No one can prove that something really happened billions of
28 years ago. In the future, new information will either support this
29 theory or show that it is wrong. For now, scientists accept the im-
30 pact theory because it explains what we know today about the Earth
31 and the moon.

• A. Scanning for Information

Read the following questions. Then go back to the complete passage and scan quickly for the answers. Write them in the space under each question.

1. a. How many times did the United States send astronauts to the moon?

    1. one time
    2. three times
    3. We don't know.

   b. What did the astronauts bring back with them?

   _____

2. What kinds of information did scientists study in order to explain the origin of the moon?

   _____

   _____

   _____

3. a. Describe the **impact theory.**

_____

_____

   b. What are some facts about the Earth and the moon that this theory explains?

_____

_____

   c. How will future information affect this theory?

_____

4. What is the main idea of this passage?
   a. The Earth and the moon are the same age.
   b. The impact theory is the best explanation of the moon's origin for several reasons.
   c. Scientists have developed different theories to explain the origin of the moon.

• B. Word Forms

In English, some verbs (v.) become nouns (n.) by adding the suffix *-tion*, for example, *educate* (v.), *education* (n.). Sometimes there are spelling changes, too. Read the following sentences. Decide if each sentence needs a noun or a verb. Circle the correct answer.

1. The librarian <u>informed / information</u> me that the library is not
          (v.)   (n.)
    open on Sunday.

2. She gave me this <u>informed / information</u> over the telephone
              (v.)   (n.)
    yesterday morning.

3. Scientists believe that the <u>formed / formation</u> of the Earth and
                    (v.)   (n.)
    Mars happened at the same time.

4. The Earth and Mars <u>formed / formation</u> at the same time.
              (v.)   (n.)

5. Our teacher always <u>explains / explanations</u> the directions very
              (v.)   (n.)
    clearly.

6. We usually understand her <u>explains / explanations</u> .
                  (v.)   (n.)

7. Drug companies frequently <u>create / creation</u> new medicines.
                  (v.)   (n.)

8. The <u>create / creation</u> of these new medicines takes a long time.
        (v.)   (n.)

• C. Vocabulary in Context

Read the following sentences. Choose the correct answer for each sentence. Write your answer in the blank space.

development (n.)   **guess** (n.)   **support** (v.)   **wonder** (v.)

1. Henry told me his _____ about the origin of all the planets.

2. Many people _____ if there is life on other planets, such as Mars.

3. I know that the _____ of useful theories is very important.

4. Some scientific tests _____ Albert Einstein's theories about time.

for now   **in the future**   **then**

5. Travel to other planets is not possible right now, but _____ astronauts may travel to Mars or other planets.

6. Matt is only 14, so he has to ride his bicycle to school _____. However, when he becomes 17, he will be able to drive a car to school.

7. I plan to live in New York until I graduate from college. _____ I will move back to my country.

but (conj.)   **finally** (adv.)   **perhaps**

8. We wanted to go on vacation, but we didn't have enough money. We saved our money for two years, and we were _____ able to take a long vacation.

9. Max called Joyce on the telephone last night, _____ she wasn't home. He'll try to speak with her again today.

10. I don't know the directions to the bank. _____ my sister can give you that information. She knows the city very well.

• D. Follow-up Activities

1. Work with two or three people. Your group is going to send a spacecraft into space. Decide where it will go. Why do you want the spacecraft to go there? What do you want to find out about this place? Write your group's plan on the blackboard. Compare all the groups' plans. As a class, vote on which plan is best.

2. Some countries, such as the United States and Russia, are planning to build stations on the planet Mars. People will live and work there. Work with a group. Discuss the advantages and disadvantages of living on Mars. Make a list of both, and compare these with your other classmates. Decide if it is a good idea to send people to Mars to live and work.

• E. Topics for Discussion and Writing

1. Do you think it is important to study the moon and the planets? Why or why not? Write a paragraph describing your reasons.

2. Write in your journal. Some groups of people believe that there may be life on other planets. They are searching for signs of life. Do you agree that there may be life on other planets? Why or why not?

• F. Crossword Puzzle

Across

3. Scientists _____ the moon came from the Earth, but they do not have proof.
5. Scientists study the _____ of the moon around the Earth.
6. The sun is very _____, but the Earth is not.
7. The opposite of **no**
9. The moon is the brightest _____ in the night sky.
10. The opposite of **yes**
12. When we look _____ at the sky, we see the sun, the stars, the moon, and planets.
13. The distance _____ the Earth to the moon is about 250,000 miles.
15. New information may _____, or help prove, the scientists' belief.
18. The scientists may be _____, or incorrect.
19. Many scientists believe that the moon _____ from the Earth.
22. The past of **put**
23. People have several _____, or guesses, about the origin of the moon.
26. When a rock hits something hard, it can break into _____.
27. Astronomers are _____ who study the stars and planets.
29. The Earth and the moon are both about 4.5 _____ years old.

Down

1. The Earth has iron in its _____, or middle.
2. Scientists _____ a lot of information about the Earth and the moon.
3. Scientists believe that a large object hit the Earth and _____ into many pieces.
4. Scientists need more _____ about the Earth and the moon.
5. The Earth has one _____, but Mars has two.
6. Scientists believe that a large object _____ the Earth many millions of years ago.
8. We need a lot of information in order to _____ something that happened a long time ago.
11. The path, or route, that the moon takes around the Earth is called an _____.
14. When one objects hits another object, it _____, or makes, heat.
15. **He, _____, it**
16. Scientists cannot _____ their theory. They can only say that evidence supports it.
17. maybe; possibly
20. When an object hits something, this is called an _____.
21. People look up _____ the moon and think about it.
24. Scientists ask questions about the _____ of the moon. They also ask how the Earth was formed.
25. The present of **ate**
28. The _____ is the brightest object in the sky during the day.
30. The Earth _____ the only planet we know that has life.

• G. Cloze Quiz

Read the following paragraphs. Fill in each space with the correct word from the list. Use each word only once.

around	dry	heat	moon	pieces
believe	**facts**	**large**	**object**	**time**

Today most scientists (1)_____ that the moon formed from the Earth. They think that a (2)_____ object hit the Earth. Perhaps the (3)_____ was as big as Mars. When the object hit the Earth, huge (4)_____ of the Earth broke off. These pieces went into orbit (5)_____ the Earth. After a brief (6)_____ , the pieces came to-gether and formed the (7)_____ . This "impact theory" explains many (8)_____ about the Earth and the moon. For example, the moon is very (9)_____ because the impact created so much (10)_____ that it dried up all the water.

center	either	however	same	theory
Earth	**future**	**prove**	**scientists**	**wrong**

The Earth has iron in its center. (11)_____ , the moon has very little iron in its (12)_____ . The moon formed from lighter materials that make up the outer part of the (13)_____ . Finally, the Earth and the moon are almost the (14)_____ age: about 4.5 billion years old.

No one can (15)_____ that something really hap-pened billions of years ago. In the (16)_____ , new in-formation will (17)_____ support this theory or show that it is (18)_____ . For now, (19)_____ accept the impact (20)_____ because it explains what we know today about the Earth and the moon.

C·H·A·P·T·E·R 10

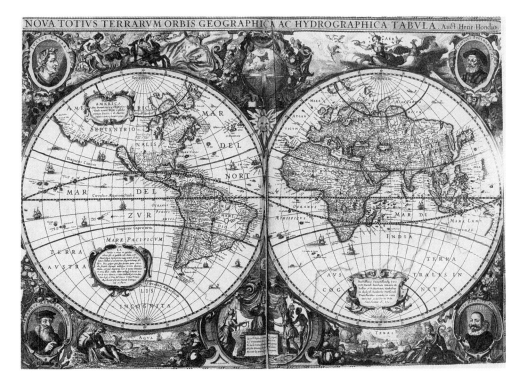

1636 Mercator World Map

Maps:
The Keys to Our World

1. What is a map? Work in a small group. Write a definition of **map**. Write it in the box below. Then look up the word **map** in your dictionary. Write the dictionary definition in the box. Compare your definition with the dictionary's.

Your Definition of MAP	Dictionary Definition of MAP

147

2. Work in your group. Make a list of the different types of maps and their different uses.

Type of Map	Uses of this Type of Map
1. a street map	to help people find houses, stores, museums, or other buildings in a city
2.	
3.	
4.	
5.	

3. Read the title of this passage. How can maps be keys to our world? In other words, what do you think this passage will be about?

Directions: Read each paragraph carefully. Then answer the questions.

Maps: The Keys to Our World

We have street maps, bus maps, train maps, and road maps. We have maps of our countries, maps of the oceans, and maps of the world. We even have maps of other planets, such as Venus and Mars. These modern maps are very useful and important to us today, but maps are not a new invention. In fact, people have made and used maps for centuries.

1. People have made maps of everything: streets, countries, oceans, and planets. Why are maps so important to us? What do you think?

   _____

2. Modern maps are very useful and important to us today. **In fact**, people have made and used maps for centuries. What is the purpose of **in fact?**

   a. **In fact** introduces new information.
   b. **In fact** shows that the previous sentence is true.
   c. **In fact** shows that information is repeated.

3. What did maps look like hundreds of years ago? In other words, how were they different from maps we have today?

   _____

4. When do you think people began to make maps?

   _____ years ago

In Iraq, archaeologists discovered maps that are over 4,300 years old. These maps were made of clay. In China, archaeologists discovered silk maps that are 2,000 years old. However, historians believe that mapmaking in China is much older than 2,000 years. All these maps represented small areas, for example, farmland and towns.

Archaeologists believe that the first map of the world may be a 2,600-year-old clay map from Babylonia (in modern Iraq). Ancient people did not know what the world really looked like, but they had many ideas about it. The Babylonian map shows the Earth as a flat circle. The circle contains a huge ocean with several islands in it. Other ancient maps showed the Earth on the back of a turtle, with four elephants holding the Earth up.

5. Archaeologists are people who

    a. have many ideas about what the world looks like
    b. study the life and culture of people who lived in the past
    c. make maps of the world from clay and silk

6. Historians believe that mapmaking in China is much older than 2,000 years. If this is true, why do you think historians didn't find older maps in China, but they did find older maps in Iraq?

    _____

7. Why did the oldest maps represent farms and towns? Why didn't the oldest maps represent the world? What do you think?

    _____

8. Read the ideas that ancient people had about the Earth. What did these people believe?

    a. They believed that the Earth was round.
    b. They believed that the Earth was flat.

9. What do you think the next paragraph will be about?

    _____

For centuries, people wondered how big the Earth was. Unfortunately, as long as they thought the Earth was flat, no one was able to figure out its size. Gradually, however, people began to realize that the Earth was really round.

Then, in the third century B.C. (2,300 years ago), a Greek man named Eratosthenes had an idea. Eratosthenes was sure that the Earth was a sphere. He used the sun and geometry to figure out the size of the Earth. He calculated that the circumference of the Earth was 28,600 miles (46,000 kilometers). The true size of the Earth is 25,000 miles (40,000 kilometers). Eratosthenes' measurement was wrong, but it was very close to the truth.

10. **As long as** people thought the Earth was flat, no one was able to **figure out** its size.

    a. **As long as** means

        1. very long
        2. the same size
        3. while

    b. **Figure out** means

        1. draw
        2. learn
        3. take out

11. **Gradually** means

    a. very slowly
    b. after 100 years
    c. scientifically

12. A **sphere** is a

    a. large shape
    b. planet
    c. ball

13. Eratosthenes used the sun and geometry to **figure out** the size of the Earth. He calculated that the circumference of the Earth was 46,000 kilometers.

    a. What is a synonym for **figure out**?

        1. geometry
        2. kilometer
        3. calculate

b. Look at the three drawings below. Which one shows the circumference of the Earth?

1.

2.

3.

14. A **measurement** is a

  a. calculation
  b. kilometer
  c. true statement

For many centuries after Eratosthenes lived, people made maps of
the Earth. However, they did not know very much about the world
outside of Europe, Asia, and north Africa. Mapmakers could not draw
accurate maps of the Earth until people began traveling around the
world in the fifteenth century, mapping small areas each time. In the
eighteenth and nineteenth centuries, people began making correct
maps of countries, but the first accurate maps of the world were not
made until the 1890s.

Maps today are reliable, inexpensive, and easy to understand.
People depend on maps every day. What would our lives be like without them?

15. Why didn't people know much about the world for such a long
time?

_____

16. **Accurate** means

  a. big
  b. small
  c. correct

17. The fifteenth century is

  a. the time from 1401 to 1500
  b. the time from 1501 to 1600

18. How did people begin to learn about the world outside Europe,
Asia, and north Africa?

  a. They took photographs of the other parts of the world.
  b. People lived in other parts of the world.
  c. People traveled and made maps of different areas.

Model of Babylonian Clay Tablet

Directions: Read the complete passage. When you are finished, you will answer the questions that follow.

Maps: The Keys to Our World

1 We have street maps, bus maps, train maps, and road maps. We
2 have maps of our countries, maps of the oceans, and maps of the
3 world. We even have maps of other planets, such as Venus and
4 Mars. These modern maps are very useful and important to us to-
5 day, but maps are not a new invention. In fact, people have made
6 and used maps for centuries.

7 In Iraq, archaeologists discovered maps that are over 4,300 years
8 old. These maps were made of clay. In China, archaeologists discov-
9 ered silk maps that are 2,000 years old. However, historians believe
10 that mapmaking in China is much older than 2,000 years. All these
11 maps represented small areas, for example, farmland and towns.

12 Archaeologists believe that the first map of the world may be a
13 2,600-year-old clay map from Babylonia (in modern Iraq). Ancient
14 people did not know what the world really looked like, but they had
15 many ideas about it. The Babylonian map shows the Earth as a flat
16 circle. The circle contains a huge ocean with several islands in it.
17 Other ancient maps showed the Earth on the back of a turtle, with
18 four elephants holding the Earth up.

19   For centuries, people wondered how big the Earth was. Unfortu-
20 nately, as long as they thought the Earth was flat, no one was able
21 to figure out its size. Gradually, however, people began to realize
22 that the Earth was really round.
23   Then, in the third century B.C. (2,300 years ago), a Greek man
24 named Eratosthenes had an idea. Eratosthenes was sure that the
25 Earth was a sphere. He used the sun and geometry to figure out the
26 size of the Earth. He calculated that the circumference of the Earth
27 was 28,600 miles (46,000 kilometers). The true size of the Earth is
28 25,000 miles (40,000 kilometers). Eratosthenes' measurement was
29 wrong, but it was very close to the truth.
30   For many centuries after Eratosthenes lived, people made maps
31 of the Earth. However, they did not know very much about the
32 world outside of Europe, Asia, and north Africa. Mapmakers could
33 not draw accurate maps of the Earth until people began traveling
34 around the world in the fifteenth century, mapping small areas each
35 time. In the eighteenth and nineteenth centuries, people began
36 making correct maps of countries, but the first accurate maps of
37 the world were not made until the 1890s.
38   Maps today are reliable, inexpensive, and easy to understand.
39 People depend on maps every day. What would our lives be like
40 without them?

• A. Scanning for Information

Read the following questions. Then go back to the complete passage
and scan quickly for the answers. Write them in the space under each
question.

1. What are some map discoveries that archaeologists have made?

   a. _____

   b. _____

   c. _____

2. In the past, what shape did most people think the Earth had?

   _____

3. Describe the first map of the world.

   _____

4. a. Who calculated the circumference of the Earth?

   _____

   b. When?

   _____

   c. What did he think the circumference of the Earth was?

   _____

   d. Was his calculation correct?

   _____

5. When were the first reliable maps of the world made?

   _____

6. What is the main idea of this passage?

   a. The first maps were made thousands of years ago.
   b. Throughout time, maps have been important to people around the world.
   c. Maps are important to people today because they are very accurate.

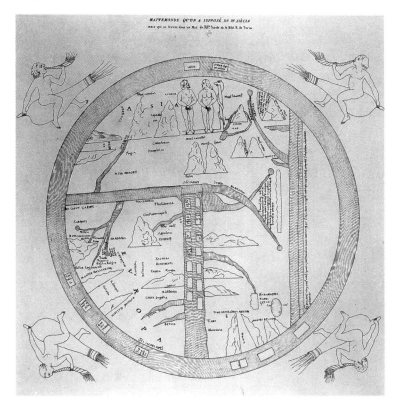

Tenth Century European Map of the World

• B. Word Forms

In English, almost all adjectives become adverbs by adding the suffix *-ly*, for example, *correct* (adj.), *correctly* (adv.). Read the sentences. Decide if each sentence needs an adjective or an adverb. Circle the correct answer.

1. Years ago, cars were not <u>reliable / reliably</u>. They
                    (adj.)   (adv.)

   broke down often.

2. However, cars perform very <u>reliable / reliably</u> today.
                 (adj.)   (adv.)

3. You can eat <u>inexpensive / inexpensively</u> at the new
            (adj.)   (adv.)

   Italian restaurant.

4. The restaurant offers very <u>inexpensive / inexpensively</u>
                 (adj.)   (adv.)

   lunches and dinners on its menu.

5. Road maps are <u>easy / easily</u> to read.
         (adj.) (adv.)

6. We can use road maps very <u>easy / easily</u>.
                (adj.) (adv.)

7. Suzanne did her math calculations <u>accurate / accurately</u>.
                 (adj.)   (adv.)

8. She is always <u>accurate / accurately</u> with her figures.
         (adj.)   (adv.)

• C. Vocabulary in Context

Read the following sentences. Choose the correct answer for each sentence. Write your answer in the blank space.

gradually (adv.)   **in fact**   **unfortunately** (adv.)

1. Burt wants to go to the movies with us tonight.
   _____, he has to stay home and study for a math test.

2. I enjoy collecting old maps. _____, I have about 200 old maps in my collection.

3. Tina practiced the piano every day. _____, she became a very good pianist.

as long as   **however**   **until**

4. We want to write a composition. _____, we don't have any paper.

5. Harry never stops working _____ he finishes a job.

6. The children can play outside _____ it is daylight. They have to come inside in the evening.

calculated (v.)   **realized** (v.)   **wondered** (v.)

7. Ann left the party early. Bill _____ why she didn't stay later. He'll ask her tomorrow.

8. The computer _____ the answer more quickly than I did.

9. Ann _____ that the TV was broken when she tried to turn it on.

• D. Follow-up Activities

1. Refer to the list of maps and their uses that you made at the beginning of this chapter.

   a. What uses of maps did you write that are not mentioned in the first paragraph?
   b. What uses of maps are in the first paragraph but not on your list? Write these on your list.

2. The passage states that people began to realize that the Earth was really round. What do you think made people understand that the Earth was really round? Make a list of ideas or clues, that you think helped people decide that the Earth was really round.

   a. _____

   b. _____

   c. _____

   d. _____

• E. Topics for Discussion and Writing

1. At the end of the reading, the author says that people depend on maps every day. Work with a partner. Make a list of the ways that people depend on maps. Compare your list with your classmates' lists. How many different ways do people depend on maps?

2. Write in your journal. At the end of the reading, the author asks what our lives would be like without maps. Describe an experience you had when you needed a map but didn't have one. Where were you? What happened? Write a paragraph about this event. When you are finished, work with one or two classmates. Read each other's stories. Decide whose experience was the most frightening, the funniest, or the most interesting. Then compare each group's favorite experience. As a class, decide on the most interesting experience.

• F. Crossword Puzzle

Across

1. Six hundred years ago, people thought that the Earth was _____, not round.
5. At first, people made maps of small _____ that they were familiar with.
7. Scientists _____ maps made of clay and silk.
8. We can buy maps of cities, countries, _____ the world.
10. slowly, over time
12. Eratosthenes tried to _____ out the size of the Earth.
13. each; every
16. Eratosthenes used geometry in order to _____ the size of the Earth.
17. The Earth is a _____, or ball.
20. **Me, her, _____, it, us, you, them**
21. Today, maps are very _____, or correct.
22. the past of **do**
24. We have _____ of the Earth, the moon, and some of the planets.
26. It is a _____ that the Earth is round.
27. Maps do not cost a lot of money. They are _____.
31. Babylonia is in the _____-day country of Iraq.
32. the past of **say**

Down

2. _____ are people who study past human life and culture.
3. the past of **have**
4. Maps _____ areas of the Earth such as cities.
6. to understand; to _____
9. dependable
11. the opposite of **down**
12. The Earth is round. The Earth orbits the sun. These are _____.
14. We have maps of other planets, such _____ Mars and Venus.
15. A circumference is a _____ of a round shape such as a ball.
18. Before photography, people used to _____ maps.
19. We _____ make very detailed maps today.
23. People rely on, or _____ on, maps every day.
24. **I, _____; she, her; he, him**
25. The Earth, Mars, and Venus are all _____.
28. the past of **put**
29. The maps we have today are _____ detailed.
30. It is _____ true that the Earth sits on the back of a turtle.

• G. Cloze Clues

Read the following paragraphs. Fill in each space with the correct word from the list. Use each word ony once.

ancient	countries	first	invention	planets
centuries	even	ideas	maps	useful

We have street maps, bus maps, train (1)_____ , and road maps. We have maps of our (2)_____ , maps of the oceans, and maps of the world. We (3)_____ have maps of other (4)_____ , such as Venus and Mars. These modern maps are very (5)_____ and important to us today, but maps are not a new (6)_____ . In fact, people have made and used maps for (7)_____ . Archaeologists believe that the (8)_____ map of the world may be a 2,600-year-old clay map from Babylonia (in modern Iraq). (9)_____ people did not know what the world really looked like, but they had many (10)_____ about it.

accurate	began	draw	not	until
around	depend	inexpensive	time	without

Mapmakers could not (11) _____ accurate maps of the Earth (12) _____ people began traveling (13)_____ the world in the fifteenth century, mapping small areas each (14)_____ . In the eighteenth and nineteenth centuries, people (15)_____ making correct maps of countries, but the first (16)_____ maps of the world were (17)_____ made until the 1890s.

Maps today are reliable, (18)_____ , and easy to understand. People (19)_____ on maps every day. What would our lives be like (20)_____ them?

Future Technology Today

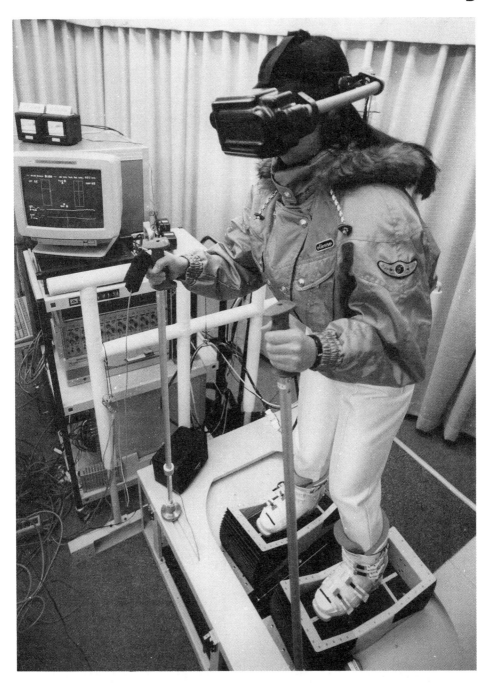

C·H·A·P·T·E·R 11

Saving Lives with Weather Forecasting

• Prereading Preparation

1. What is weather forecasting? Who does it?

2. Look at the picture on the left. Work with a partner. What do you think happens to buildings when a tornado strikes? What are its effects? Describe them. Compare your description with your classmates' answers.

3. Read the title of this chapter. What do you think this passage will discuss?

Directions: Read each paragraph carefully. Then answer the questions.

Saving Lives with Weather Forecasting

On the night of April 25, 1994, a massive tornado struck the town of Lancaster, Texas. The tornado destroyed more than 175 homes. It also flattened the business district. Ordinarily, a tornado like the one that struck Lancaster kills dozens of people. Amazingly, only four people died.

1. **Massive** means

   a. destroy
   b. very big
   c. windy

2. _____ True _____ False   The tornado destroyed the business district.

3. **Ordinarily** means

   a. usually
   b. really
   c. obviously

4. **Amazingly, only four people died.** This sentence means

   a. it is good that only four people died
   b. it is surprising that only four people died
   c. it is sad that four people died

Why did so few people die that night in Lancaster? Part of the reason is modern weather technology: **Next Generation Weather Radar**, or **Nexrad**. This sphere-shaped instrument identified the tornado a full 40 minutes before the tornado hit. As a result, weather forecasters were able to warn the people in the town. This advance warning helped many people to leave Lancaster before the tornado struck.

Nexrad is the first weather-service radar that can detect strong winds and rain, which are characteristic of severe thunderstorms and tornadoes. In the past, an obsolete radar system was used to predict such storms. Under this old system, warnings often depended on eyewitness reports. These reports gave people only about three minutes to prepare for the tornado.

5. What is **Nexrad**?

_____

6. This advance warning helped many people to leave Lancaster before the tornado struck. **Advance warning** means

   a. to warn people before something happens
   b. to warn people after something happens

7. _____ True _____ False   Two characteristics of thunderstorms and tornadoes are wind and rain.

8. **Characteristic** means

   a. wind or rain
   b. reason or cause
   c. quality or trait

9. **Obsolete** means

   a. not useful
   b. very new
   c. very useful

Today, more than 100 Nexrad systems are in place in the United States. By the late 1990s, a total of 152 systems will be working throughout the country. In the past, many severe thunderstorms and tornadoes struck without warning. Weather forecasters could not predict all of them. In fact, they did not predict 33 percent of all thunderstorms and tornadoes. As a result of Nexrad, this percent has decreased to 13 percent. When all the Nexrad systems are in place, this percentage will be even lower.

10. What years are **the late 1990s**?

    a. 1990–1993
    b. 1993–1996
    c. 1997–1999

11. How many Nexrad systems will be in place by the late 1990s?

_____

12. As a result of Nexrad, this percent has decreased to 13 percent. **Decrease** means

    a. become higher
    b. become lower
    c. stay the same

Tornadoes occur all over the world, but most often in the United States. One third of all U.S. tornadoes strike in Oklahoma, Texas, and Kansas. Alaska is the only state that has never had a tornado. A tornado may last from several seconds to several hours, and its winds may reach up to 300 miles per hour (500 kilometers per hour). Because tornadoes are so powerful and so destructive, it is important to be able to predict them accurately. Consequently, the Nexrad system will become an indispensable part of American weather forecasting.

13. _____ True _____ False   Tornadoes occur only in the United States.

14. _____ True _____ False   Tornadoes may last a short time or a long time.

15. Because tornadoes are so powerful and so destructive, it is important to be able to predict them accurately. **Accurately** means

   a. exactly
   b. carefully
   c. early

16. **Indispensable** means

   a. useful
   b. important
   c. necessary

17. **Consequently** means

   a. however
   b. as a result
   c. hopefully

Directions: Read the complete passage. When you are finished, you will answer the questions that follow.

Saving Lives with Weather Forecasting

1   On the night of April 25, 1994, a massive tornado struck the
2 town of Lancaster, Texas. The tornado destroyed more than 175
3 homes. It also flattened the business district. Ordinarily, a tornado
4 like the one that struck Lancaster kills dozens of people. Amaz-
5 ingly, only four people died.
6   Why did so few people die that night in Lancaster? Part of the
7 reason is modern weather technology: Next Generation Weather Ra-
8 dar, or Nexrad. This sphere-shaped instrument identified the tor-
9 nado a full 40 minutes before the tornado hit. As a result, weather
10 forecasters were able to warn the people in the town. This advance
11 warning helped many people to leave Lancaster before the tornado
12 struck.
13   Nexrad is the first weather-service radar that can detect strong
14 winds and rain, which are characteristic of severe thunderstorms
15 and tornadoes. In the past, an obsolete radar system was used to
16 predict such storms. Under this old system, warnings often de-
17 pended on eyewitness reports. These reports gave people only
18 about three minutes to prepare for the tornado.
19   Today, more than 100 Nexrad systems are in place in the United
20 States. By the late 1990s, a total of 152 systems will be working
21 throughout the country. In the past, many severe thunderstorms
22 and tornadoes struck without warning. Weather forecasters could
23 not predict all of them. In fact, they did not predict 33 percent of
24 all thunderstorms and tornadoes. As a result of Nexrad, this percent
25 has decreased to 13 percent. When all the Nexrad systems are in
26 place, this percentage will be even lower.
27   Tornadoes occur all over the world, but most often in the United
28 States. One third of all U.S. tornadoes strike in Oklahoma, Texas,
29 and Kansas. Alaska is the only state that has never had a tornado. A
30 tornado may last from several seconds to several hours, and its
31 winds may reach up to 300 miles per hour (500 kilometers per
32 hour). Because tornadoes are so powerful and so destructive, it is
33 important to be able to predict them accurately. Consequently, the
34 Nexrad system will become an indispensable part of American
35 weather forecasting.

• A. Scanning for Information

Read the following questions. Then go back to the complete passage
and scan quickly for the answers. Write them in the space under each
question.

1. In lines 4 and 5, why was it amazing that only four people
   died?

   _____

   _____

2. How did Nexrad save lives?

   _____

   _____

3. Before Nexrad, how did many forecasters know that a tornado
   was coming?

   _____

   _____

4. Is it important to accurately predict tornadoes? Why or why not?

   _____

   _____

5. What is the main idea of this passage?
   a. Tornadoes occur all over the world, but most tornadoes
      strike the United States.
   b. There is a new weather system that can predict tornadoes
      and save lives.
   c. A massive tornado struck a town in Texas, but only four
      people died.

• B. Word Forms

In English, some verbs (v.) become nouns (n.) by adding *-ence* or *-ance*. Read the sentences below. Decide if each sentence needs a verb or a noun. Circle the correct answer.

1. Carmen <u>avoided / avoidance</u> alcohol while she was pregnant.
            (v.)   (n.)

2. <u>Avoid / Avoidance</u> of alcohol is important for a healthy baby.
   (v.)   (n.)

3. Tornadoes are a rare <u>occur / occurrence</u> in New Jersey.
               (v.)   (n.)

4. They rarely <u>occur / occurrence</u> in Hawaii, too.
          (v.)   (n.)

5. Joanne's <u>depends / dependence</u> on her car is a problem.
        (v.)   (n.)

6. Joanne even <u>depends / dependence</u> on her car to drive three
           (v.)   (n.)
blocks to the store.

7. Some buildings <u>resist / resistance</u> high winds.
          (v.)   (n.)

8. This wind <u>resist / resistance</u> can save lives during a tornado.
       (v.)   (n.)

• C. Vocabulary in Context

Read the following sentences. Choose the correct answer for each sentence. Write your answer in the blank space.

indispensable (adj.)   **obsolete** (adj.)   **severe** (adj.)

1. Because most businesses use computers, typewriters have become _____.

2. Computers are _____ to most businesses. They could not operate without computers!

3. Danielle has a _____ cold. Her doctor told her to stay in bed for several days.

accurately (adv.)   **amazingly** (adv.)   **consequently** (adv.)

4. Kristen did not study last night. _____, she was not prepared for the exam this morning.

5. My wristwatch keeps time _____. It is now exactly noon.

6. I saw a terrible car accident on the highway. _____, no one was hurt.

decreases (v.)   **destroyed** (v.)   **predicts** (v.)   **warned** (v.)

7. As the temperature _____, the weather becomes colder.

8. The weather forecaster _____ a warm, sunny day for tomorrow. Let's all go to the beach!

9. Christina's mother _____ her not to play near the street.

10. During the thunderstorm, a huge tree fell and _____ my car.

• D. Follow-up Activities

1. The following illustration shows how tornadoes are formed.
   Look at the four steps carefully. Then put the four descriptions
   in the correct order.

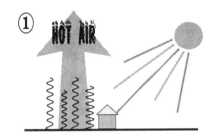

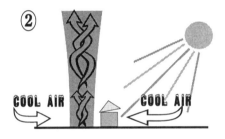

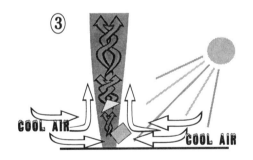

_____ Cooler air nearby rushes in to fill the space left by the rising
hot air.

_____ As the Earth rotates, it causes the rotating motion in the air
column. This process becomes stronger.

_____ The sun heats the ground. Columns of hot air rise where the
ground is the hottest.

_____ This process speeds up and increases. It generates extremely
high winds.

2. Tornadoes occur mostly in the United States. Work with a partner from your country. What kinds of severe weather (for example, hurricanes, typhoons, floods, blizzards) happen in your country? Make a list. Then write it on the blackboard. Join your country's list with other countries' lists. Make a chart of all the countries' severe weather.

3. It is important to be able to predict tornadoes in order to save lives. What other occurrences is it important to be able to predict? Work with two or three classmates. Make a list. Compare it with your other classmates' lists.

• E. Topics for Discussion and Writing

1. Nexrad is an important system because it can save lives. Think about another invention (for example, a smoke detector) that can save lives. Describe this invention. What does it do? Write a paragraph about it.

2. Many people listen to the weather forecast every day. Do you listen to it also? Why or why not? Do you think it is necessary every day? Write a paragraph about this.

3. Write in your journal. Did you ever experience severe weather (tornadoes, snowstorms, floods, etc.)? Write about this experience. If you did not experience bad weather yourself, write about what you read in a newspaper or heard about on television or radio.

• F. Crossword Puzzle

Across

1. Nexrad is a weather predicting _____ in the United States.
4. We _____ studying English.
6. We enjoy warm, sunny _____.
8. the past of **do**
11. The number of deaths from plane accidents has _____ recently. That's good news!
13. Modern technology is an _____ part of our lives. We cannot live and work without it.
16. Severe storms can be very _____. They flatten buildings and kill people.
18. Weather _____ are people who try to predict storms and other bad weather.
19. every; each
21. the opposite of **no**
22. Many people try to _____ the future. They try to tell what will happen.
23. the present of **ate**
24. I am _____ that it will rain tomorrow. I am certain.

Down

1. New York is a _____ in the United States. California is a _____, too.
2. Nexrad is shaped like a _____. The Earth and the moon are this shape, too.
3. **I, _____; he, him; she, her; we, us**
5. Nexrad means "Next Generation Weather _____."
6. We heard a _____ on the radio that a severe thunderstorm is coming.
7. the past of **have**
9. _____, most people don't work on Saturday and Sunday in the United States.
10. John _____ speak two languages.
12. An airplane crashed in the mountains last night. _____, no one was killed.
14. We are coming to the _____ of this book. The next chapter is the last chapter.
15. Nexrad is very _____, or correct.
17. _____ are very powerful; they can destroy trees and buildings in a few minutes.
18. After a severe storm, some areas may be completely _____ because the buildings were destroyed.
20. Certain types of storms _____ only in particular parts of the world.
22. the past of **put**

• G. Cloze Clues

Read the following paragraphs. Fill in each space with the correct word from the list. Use each word only once.

> **characteristic   late   obsolete   predict   severe**
> **eyewitness   lower   percentage   prepare   warning**

Nexrad can detect strong winds and rain, which are (1)_____ of severe thunderstorms and tornadoes. In the past, an (2)_____ radar system was used to predict such storms. Under this old system, warnings often depended on (3)_____ reports. These reports gave people only about three minutes to (4)_____ for the tornado.

   Today, more than 100 Nexrad systems are in place in the United States. By the (5)_____ 1990s, a total of 152 systems will be working throughout the country. In the past, many (6)_____ thunderstorms and tornadoes struck without (7)_____ . Weather forecasters could not (8)_____ all of them. In fact, they did not predict 33 percent of all thunderstorms and tornadoes. As a result of Nexrad, this (9)_____ has decreased to 13 percent. When all the Nexrad systems are in place, this percentage will be even (10)_____ .

> **accurately   destructive   indispensable   only   tornado**
> **all   hour   occur   several   weather**

   Tornadoes (11)_____ all over the world, but most often in the United States. One third of (12)_____ U.S. tornadoes strike in Oklahoma, Texas, and Kansas. Alaska is the (13)_____ state that has never had a (14)_____ . A tornado may last from several seconds to (15)_____ hours, and its winds may reach up to 300 miles per (16)_____ (500 kilometers per hour). Because tornadoes are so powerful and so (17)_____ , it is important to be able to predict them (18)_____ . Consequently, the Nexrad system will become an (19)_____ part of American (20)_____ forecasting.

C·H·A·P·T·E·R 12

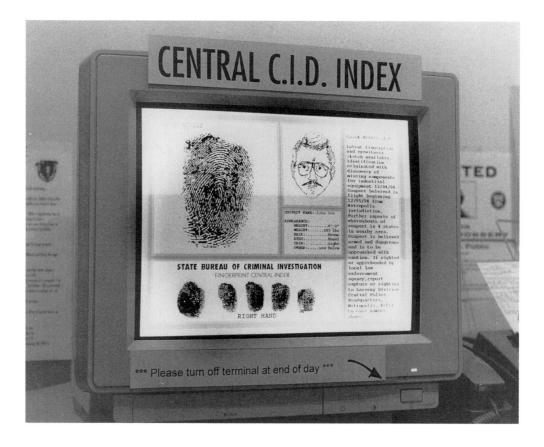

Clues and Criminal Investigation

• Prereading Preparation

1. What kinds of evidence can prove that a person committed a crime? Work with a partner. Look at the list of clues, and decide what type of crime these clues might help solve. Some clues may help solve more than one kind of crime. When you are finished, compare your work with your other classmates' work. Did you make the same decisions?

blood	dirt	hair
bullets	fingerprints	pieces of glass
clothing fibers	footprints	a ransom note

2. Think of a crime that you heard about or read about. Describe it to your partner. What clues did the police use to help them solve this crime?

3. Read the title of this passage. What do you think the reading will be about?

Directions: Read each paragraph carefully. Then answer the questions.

Clues and Criminal Investigation

If you wanted to solve a crime such as a robbery or a murder, how would you start? What types of evidence would you look for? Crime experts all have a basic principle, or belief: a criminal always brings something to the scene of a crime and always leaves something there. As a result, crime experts always begin their criminal investigation with a careful examination of the place where the crime occurred.

1. A **crime expert** is

    a. a professional at committing crimes
    b. a professional at solving crimes

2. A **principle** is

    a. an idea that you have
    b. evidence that you have
    c. a belief that you have

3. What do crime experts think?

    a. They think that criminals are usually not very careful.
    b. They think that they can solve every crime that occurs.
    c. They think that they will always find clues at the scene of a crime.

4. What do you think the next paragraph will discuss?

    _____

When criminal investigators arrive at the scene of a crime, they look for evidence, or clues, from the criminal. This evidence includes footprints, fingerprints, lip prints on glasses, hair, blood, clothing fibers, and bullet shells, for example. These are all clues that the criminal may have left behind. Some clues are taken to laboratories and analyzed. For instance, fingerprints are "lifted" from a glass, a door, or a table. They are examined and compared by computer with the millions of fingerprints on file with the police, the Federal Bureau of Investigation (FBI), and other agencies.

5. The **scene of a crime** is

    a. a part of a movie
    b. the place where the crime occurred
    c. a description of the crime

6. a. **Evidence** means

    1. clues
    2. criminals
    3. beliefs

  b. Some examples of clues are

    _____

7. Fingerprints are "lifted" from a glass, a door, or a table. Then experts analyze them in a laboratory. In the first sentence, **lifted** means

    a. found
    b. taken
    c. examined

8. What will the next part of this reading discuss?

    _____

In the case of murder, experts examine blood and compare it to the blood of the victim. If the blood isn't the victim's, then it might be the murderer's. Furthermore, experts can analyze the DNA from a person's cells, such as skin cells. Like fingerprints, each person's DNA is unique, which means that everyone's DNA is different. These clues help to identify the criminal.

In some cases, a criminal uses a gun when committing a crime. Every gun leaves distinctive marks on a bullet when the gun is fired. The police may find a bullet at the scene or recover a bullet from a victim's body. Experts can examine the markings on the bullet and prove that it was fired from a specific gun. This clue is strong evidence that the owner of the gun may be guilty. Consequently, the police will suspect that this person committed the crime.

9. A **victim** is

   a. the person who committed a crime
   b. the person the crime is committed against

10. **Furthermore** means

   a. in addition
   b. farther away
   c. however

11. Like fingerprints, each person's DNA is **unique**, which means that everyone's DNA is different.

   a. **Unique** means
      1. from a person's body
      2. original; individual
      3. a special clue

   b. Which one of the following sentences is true?
      1. Each person's DNA and fingerprints are different from every other person's.
      2. Each person's DNA is different from every other person's, but their fingerprints are not.
      3. Each person's fingerprints are different from every other person's, but their DNA is not.

12. a. **Distinctive** means

      1. particular
      2. clear
      3. metal

    b. The markings on bullets fired from two different guns

      1. can sometimes be the same
      2. can never be the same

13. A gun's **owner** is

    a. the person who used the gun
    b. the person that the gun belongs to
    c. the person who found the gun

14. a. The police **suspect** that a person has committed a crime. This sentence means that

      1. the police are sure that a specific person has committed a crime
      2. the police believe that a specific person has committed a crime

    b. **Suspect** means

      1. think that something is true
      2. know that something is true

15. **Consequently** means

    a. in addition
    b. however
    c. as a result

Clues from the scene of a crime help the police identify a suspect. If other evidence supports these clues, then the police can charge the suspect with the crime. It is important to remember, however, that in the United States, a person is innocent until proven guilty in a court of law.

16. The police charge a person with a crime when

    a. they find a gun that belongs to that person
    b. they have blood and bullets from the scene of the crime
    c. they have evidence to show that the person may have committed the crime

17. a. The words **innocent** and **guilty**

    1. have opposite meanings
    2. have the same meaning

  b. An **innocent** person
    1. committed a crime
    2. did not commit a crime

  c. A **guilty** person

    1. committed a crime
    2. did not commit a crime

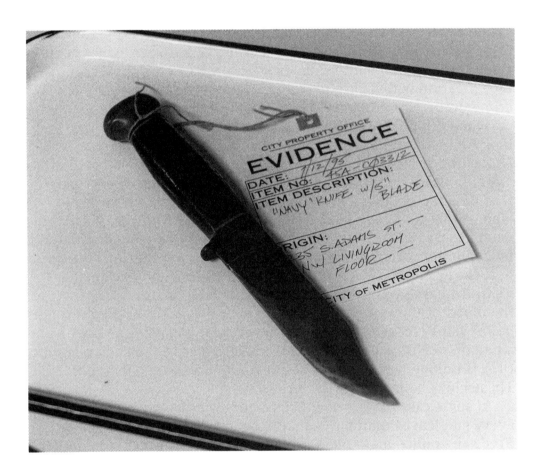

Directions: Read the complete passage. When you are finished, you will answer the questions that follow.

Clues and Criminal Investigation

1   If you wanted to solve a crime such as a robbery or a murder,
2 how would you start? What types of evidence would you look for?
3 Crime experts all have a basic principle, or belief: a criminal always
4 brings something to the scene of a crime and always leaves some-
5 thing there. As a result, crime experts always begin their criminal
6 investigation with a careful examination of the place where the
7 crime occurred.
8   When criminal investigators arrive at the scene of a crime, they
9 look for evidence, or clues, from the criminal. This evidence in-
10 cludes footprints, fingerprints, lip prints on glasses, hair, blood,
11 clothing fibers, and bullet shells, for example. These are all clues
12 that the criminal may have left behind. Some clues are taken to
13 laboratories and analyzed. For instance, fingerprints are "lifted"
14 from a glass, a door, or a table. They are examined and compared
15 by computer with the millions of fingerprints on file with the po-
16 lice, the Federal Bureau of Investigation (FBI), and other agencies.
17   In the case of murder, experts examine blood and compare it to
18 the blood of the victim. If the blood isn't the victim's, then it might
19 be the murderer's. Furthermore, experts can analyze the DNA from
20 a person's cells, such as skin cells. Like fingerprints, each person's
21 DNA is unique, which means that everyone's DNA is different.
22 These clues help to identify the criminal.
23   In some cases, a criminal uses a gun when committing a crime.
24 Every gun leaves distinctive marks on a bullet when the gun is
25 fired. The police may find a bullet at the scene or recover a bullet
26 from a victim's body. Experts can examine the markings on the bul-
27 let and prove that it was fired from a specific gun. This clue is
28 strong evidence that the owner of the gun may be guilty. Conse-
29 quently, the police will suspect that this person committed the
30 crime.
31   Clues from the scene of a crime help the police identify a sus-
32 pect. If other evidence supports these clues, then the police can
33 charge the suspect with the crime. It is important to remember,
34 however, that in the United States, a person is innocent until
35 proven guilty in a court of law.

• A. Scanning for Information

Read the following questions. Then go back to the complete passage and scan quickly for the answers. Write them in the space under each question.

1. What do all crime experts believe?

_____

2. Why are fingerprints from the scene of a crime compared with the fingerprints on file with the police, the FBI, and other agencies?

_____

3. If the blood found at the scene of a murder isn't the victim's blood, why might it be the murderer's blood?

_____

4. Why are blood, skin, and fingerprints so important to crime experts?

_____

5. What is the main idea of this passage?
   a. Criminals often leave many clues at the scene of a crime.
   b. Fingerprints and bullets are important evidence of crimes.
   c. Crime experts analyze a variety of clues to identify criminals.

• B. Word Forms

In English, some nouns become adjectives by adding *-ful*. Read the sentences below. Decide if each sentence needs a noun (n.) or an adjective (adj.). Circle the correct answer.

1. Criminal investigators are very <u>skill / skillful</u> .
                                 (n.)   (adj.)

2. Their <u>skill / skillful</u> is very important in helping them
        (n.)   (adj.)
solve crimes.

3. Gilda is unusually <u>success / successful</u> in her career.
                (n.)   (adj.)

4. She achieved <u>success / successful</u> in only a few years.
           (n.)   (adj.)

5. Roseanne gave her elderly mother a lot of <u>help / helpful</u> when
                                        (n.)   (adj.)
she was sick.

6. Because Roseanne was so <u>help / helpful</u> to her mother,
                    (n.)   (adj.)
she felt better quickly.

7. Jerry is always very <u>care / careful</u> when he paints his house.
           (n.)   (adj.)

8. He takes a lot of <u>care / careful</u> not to spill paint on the carpets.
        (n.)   (adj.)

• C. Vocabulary in Context

Read the following sentences. Choose the correct answer for each sentence. Write your answer in the blank space.

evidence (n.)   **expert** (n.)   **principle** (n.)   **suspect** (n.)

1. Emily is the most likely _____ in the murder of her husband. The police think she may have killed him.

2. Sam is a police _____ on guns and rifles. He knows more about these weapons than anyone else in the police department.

3. A strong _____ in American law is that a person is considered innocent until proven guilty.

4. The police suspect that Jean committed the store robbery, but they don't have any _____ against her, so they have to let her go.

consequently (adv.)   **furthermore** (adv.)   **if** (conj.)

5. I would go on vacation _____ I had enough money, but I don't. Perhaps I'll take a vacation next year.

6. An eyewitness saw John steal a car. The police found the stolen car in John's garage. _____, the police arrested John and charged him with the crime.

7. I'm sure that Nelson didn't shoot Tom. Nelson and Tom are very good friends. Someone else's fingerprints were on the gun. _____, Nelson was out of town on business when Tom was shot.

investigated (v.)   **occurred** (v.)   **suspected** (v.)

8. When the FBI _____ the bank robbery, they found out that the robbers had left the country.

9. Ten murders _____ in Johnston City last year.

10. Everyone _____ that Fran had a lot of money, but no one was able to prove it.

• D. Follow-up Activities

1. Work with two or three partners. Imagine that you are a group of crime experts. The police have asked you to investigate the following crimes. What clues will you look for at the scene of each crime? What additional evidence will you try to get in order to identify a suspect for each of these crimes?

Type of Crime	Clues at the Scene of the Crime	Additional Evidence
a murder		
a kidnapping		
a house break-in		
a jewelry store robbery		

2. Work with one or two partners. Make up a crime, and devise some evidence to leave "at the scene of the crime." Then have your classmates investigate your crime and try to solve it. When you have all finished, discuss your evidence. Which group had the best clues?

• E. Topics for Discussion and Writing

1. Work with two or three partners. Find a description of a crime in a book, magazine, or newspaper. Read the description of the crime, the clues, and the suspect. Decide if there is enough evidence to show this person is guilty in a court of law. Write a paragraph describing your decision. Then read another group's crime description and let them read your group's. After you have made a decision, meet with the other group. Read each other's paragraphs. Does your group agree or disagree with the other group's decisions about the two crimes? Discuss your decisions.

2. Write in your journal. Think about a crime you read about. Describe the crime. What happened? When and where did this crime take place? How did the police investigate it? What clues did they find? How did they solve the crime? Share your story with a classmate. Which crime was more difficult to solve? Why?

• F. Crossword Puzzle

Across

1. A gun leaves particular markings on a _____.
6. My dog has _____ markings. He has a black leg, a black ear, and a black spot on his head.
11. I have a very simple _____, or belief: I try my best with everything I do.
13. The police may ask many different _____ for help to solve a crime: chemists, dentists, etc.
15. We _____ doing a crossword puzzle.
16. John was the _____ of a robbery yesterday. Someone robbed him on the street.
18. each; every
21. uncommon; unusual
22. the past of **get**
23. Experts can _____ blood, hair, clothing, and other clues to a crime.
24. Mary did not steal John's wallet. She is _____ of that crime.
27. The police have a _____ in yesterday's bank robbery. They think they know who did it.

Down

2. Everyone's fingerprints are _____. No two people have the same fingerprints.
3. Maria is studying English, and we are, _____.
4. Robert is _____ tall as Gary. They are the same height.
5. Each person's _____ is unique, just like their fingerprints.
7. sick; not well
8. the opposite of **down**
9. The lines on a person's fingers are _____.
10. Crimes _____, or take place, every day.
12. Our class ends _____ 10 o'clock.
13. The police don't have any _____, or clues, in this case yet.
14. Many specialists help the police _____ crimes.
17. The police look for clues, for _____, blood, hair, bullets, fingerprints.
19. the present tense of **said**
20. Murder, robbery, kidnapping, and car theft are all types of _____.
22. Tom was found _____ of stealing cars. The evidence against him was very strong.
25. We _____ do crossword puzzles.
26. The past of **let**

• G. Cloze Clues

Read the following paragraphs. Fill in each space with the correct word from the list. Use each word only once.

belief	case	evidence	leaves	result
careful	**crime**	**furthermore**	**occurred**	**start**

If you wanted to solve a (1) _____ such as a robbery or a murder, how would you (2) _____? What types of (3)_____ would you look for? Crime experts all have a basic principle, or (4)_____ : a criminal always brings something to the scene of a crime and always (5)_____ something there. As a (6)_____ , crime experts always begin their criminal investigation with a (7)_____ examination of the place where the crime (8)_____ . In the (9)_____ of murder, experts examine blood and compare it to the blood of the victim. (10)_____ , experts can analyze the DNA from a person's cells, such as skin cells.

bullet	consequently	guilty	scene	suspect
clues	**experts**	**gun**	**specific**	**uses**

In some cases, a criminal (11)_____ a gun when committing a crime. Every gun leaves distinctive marks on a bullet when the (12)_____ is fired. The police may find a bullet at the (13)_____ , or recover a bullet from a victim's body. (14)_____ can examine the markings on the (15)_____ and prove that it was fired from a (16)_____ gun. This clue is strong evidence that the owner of the gun may be guilty. (17)_____ , the police will (18)_____ that this person committed the crime. All these clues may help police identify a suspect. If other evidence supports these (19)_____ , then the police can charge the suspect with the crime. It is important to remember, however, that in the United States, a person is innocent until proven (20)_____ in a court of law.

Index of Key Words and Phrases

Answer Key

Chapter 1: Sharks: Useful Hunters of the Sea

Questions after paragraphs:
1. 350 kinds
2. True
3. False
4. 50 to 60 feet long
5. 6 inches long
6. b
7. 100 million years old
8. b
9. a
10. b
11. False
12. True
13. c
14. a. at dawn, in the evening, or in the middle of the night
    b. 2
    c. 3
15. b
16. False
17. True
18. c
19. a

Exercise A

1. a. the whale shark and the dwarf shark
   b. The whale shark is very big, and the dwarf shark is very small.
   c. They are both meat eaters.
2. They eat sick fish and animals.
3. They feel vibrations in the water, and they use their eyes, too.
4. Because sharks almost never get cancer, and scientists want to find out why.
5. b

Exercise B

Example:
   a. hunt (v.)
   b. hunt (n.)
1. help (v.)
2. help (n.)
3. uses (n.)
4. use (v.)
5. move (v.)
6. move (n.)
7. sounds (v.)
8. sounds (n.)

Exercise C

1. common
2. afraid
3. For example
4. rare
5. another
6. movements
7. hunt
8. prevent
9. several
10. In fact

Exercise D

1. a. great white shark
   b. whale shark
   c. brown catshark
   d. dwarf shark
2. Answers will vary.

Exercise E

Answers will vary.

Exercise F

Across
2. night
4. are
7. all
9. eyes
11. ocean
12. can
15. movement
16. small
18. meat
20. afraid
21. yes
23. kinds
25. warm

Down
1. million
3. he
5. rare
6. see
8. sharks
10. scientists
12. cancer
13. not
14. all
17. many
19. to
20. am
22. big
24. dawn
26. me

Exercise G

1. afraid
2. Some
3. small
4. only
5. lived
6. ocean
7. They
8. eat
9. teeth
10. another

Chapter 2: A Brief History of Horses with Humans

Questions after paragraphs:
1. True
2. a
3. about 6,000 years ago
4. c
5. b
6. b
7. c
8. b
9. c
10. a
11. b
12. a
13. b
14. a
15. c
16. a
17. b
18. False
19. True
20. c

Exercise A

1. a. about 3,500 years ago
   b. in Mesopotamia
   c. for pulling chariots
2. Because people didn't have to stay in the same place. Because people were able to travel to other places.
3. Because the soldiers in other armies were on foot, and they were not able to fight a soldier on a horse.
4. Horses built roads, pulled ambulances and fire engines, and worked on farms.
5. b

Exercise B

Example:
   a. thank (v.)
   b. thankful (adj.)
1. use (v.)
2. useful (adj.)
3. helpful (adj.)
4. helps (v.)
5. careful (adj.)
6. care (v.)

Exercise C

1. travel
2. until
3. begin
4. mean
5. In fact
6. common
7. brief
8. indispensable
9. As a result

Exercise D

Answers will vary.

Exercise E

Answers will vary.

Exercise F

Across
1. food
2. common
5. Iraq
7. distant
8. indispensable
10. meat
11. of
13. build
14. hunted
16. powerful
18. fact

Down
1. foot
2. chariots
3. fire
4. at
6. brief
7. depended
9. armies
10. modern
12. people
15. useful
17. we
19. can

Exercise G

1. hunted
2. food
3. people
4. useful
5. first
6. depended
7. fact
8. railroads
9. worked
10. indispensable

Chapter 3: Learning a Second Language

Questions after paragraphs:
1. False
2. a
3. b
4. b
5. a
6. b
7. c
8. a. 3
   b. 1
9. c
10. a
11. c
12. b
13. a
14. c
15. a
16. c
17. a
18. True
19. c
20. a
21. a
22. a, c, d

Exercise A

1. a
2. three
3. a. Feel positive about learning English. For example, be patient.
   b. Practice English. For example, write in a journal every day. Another example is practice speaking English every day.
   c. Keep a record of my language learning. For example, think about what my accomplishments are and write them in my journal.
4. c

Exercise B

Example:
a. briefly (adv.)
b. brief (adj.)
1. easy (adj.)
2. easily (adv.)
3. naturally (adv.)
4. natural (adj.)
5. correct (adj.)
6. correctly (adv.)
7. gradually (adv.)
8. gradual (adj.)

Exercise C

1. risks
2. all at once
3. patient
4. gradual
5. positive
6. In other words
7. Perhaps
8. trouble
9. confidence
10. In addition

Exercise D

Answers will vary.

Exercise E

Answers will vary.

Exercise F

Across
1. patient
3. has
5. no
6. mistakes
7. he
8. journal
12. classmates
13. learn
14. record
15. late
16. confidence
17. say

Down
1. positive
2. natural
4. achievements
9. on
10. gradually
11. practice
16. can

Exercise G

1. easily
2. trouble
3. learn
4. such
5. interesting
6. positive
7. believe
8. practice
9. achievements
10. confidence

Chapter 4: Food and Culture

Questions after paragraphs:
1. a. 2
   b. 1
2. a
3. b
4. a. 3
   b. 3
5. False
6. False
7. a
8. c
9. c
10. True
11. b
12. a person who studies people's actions: what they eat and do, and their religion
13. a. Some people in Africa eat termites.
    b. Some people in Asia eat dog meat.
    c. Some people in Europe eat blood sausage.
14. A group of people who have the same customs, eat the same kinds of food, and have the same religion.
15. Because a change in our life, such as moving to a new place, might mean that the food we are used to is no longer available.
16. True
17. False
18. a
19. b

Exercise A

1. People like to eat food that they are familiar with.
2. Because they are not accustomed to it.
3. Because an animal is considered sacred, or because an animal is considered unclean.
4. Because these kinds of food are available to them.
5. a

Exercise B

Example:
- a. lights (n.)
- b. lights (v.)
1. tastes (n.)
2. tastes (v.)
3. moved (v.)
4. move (n.)
5. drink (n.)
6. drink (v.)
7. change (v.)
8. change (n.)

Exercise C

1. For instance
2. popular
3. In contrast
4. prefers
5. In other words
6. common
7. Few
8. accustomed to
9. unusual
10. strongly

Exercise D

Answers will vary.

Exercise E

Answers will vary.

Exercise F

Across
3. common
4. lunch
7. strongly
10. of
13. reasons
14. accustomed
15. have
17. culture
18. go
19. food
21. slowly
23. are
24. available
25. like

Down
1. not
2. popular
5. unusual
6. change

8. taste
9. on
11. familiar
12. religious
16. prefer
17. contrast
20. dislike
22. yes
24. all

Exercise G

1. accustomed
2. taste
3. popular
4. drink
5. contrast
6. habits
7. different
8. result
9. familiar
10. enjoy

Chapter 5: The Importance of Exercise for Children

Questions after paragraphs:
1. b
2. c
3. a
4. answers will vary.
5. c
6. b
7. Once a week.
8. False
9. a. 3
   b. 2
10. a. 1
    b. 3
11. True
12. 6
13. False
14. a. 3
    b. 2
    c. 1
15. True

Exercise A

1. He plays roller hockey, basketball, and baseball.
2. They exercise once a week for 45 minutes.
3. a. Yes
   b. They can become unhealthy.
4. c
5. c

Exercise B

Example:
  a. drink (v.)
  b. drink (n.)
  1. practices (v.)
  2. practice (n.)
  3. Exercise (n.)
  4. exercise (v.)
  5. diet (v.)
  6. diet (n.)
  7. changes (n.)
  8. changed (v.)

Exercise C

  1. at least
  2. habit
  3. In contrast
  4. regularly
  5. As a result
  6. active
  7. practice
  8. condition
  9. Therefore
  10. likely

Exercise D

Answers will vary.

Exercise E

Answers will vary.

Exercise F

Across
  1. has
  2. but
  3. sports
  5. are
  7. must
  8. diet
  10. fun
  12. physical
  15. life
  17. practice
  18. active
  19. busy

Down
  1. habits
  3. she
  4. overweight
  6. regularly

  9. exercise
  11. unhealthy
  13. contrast
  14. fitness
  16. team

Exercise G

  1. busy
  2. practices
  3. morning
  4. winter
  5. every
  6. week
  7. easy
  8. active
  9. Therefore
  10. exercise
  11. trouble
  12. unhealthy
  13. overweight
  14. believe
  15. result

Chapter 6: The New York City Marathon: A World Race

Questions after paragraphs:
  1. b
  2. False
  3. a
  4. True
  5. c
  6. a
  7. b
  8. False
  9. False
  10. False
  11. b

Exercise A

1. a. The course has changed. Now it goes through all five boroughs of the city, not just around Central Park.
   b. There used to be few people in the race, but now there are thousands of people.
2. The crowds cheer the runners. They also offer the runners cold drinks and encouragement.
3. Two people got married and then ran the race with their wedding party. Some people ran with their families. Some people ran backwards.
4. c

Exercise B

Example:
  a. agree (v.)
  b. agreement (n.)
  1. excite (v.)
  2. excitement (n.)
  3. encourage (v.)
  4. encouragement (n.)
  5. improvement (n.)
  6. improves (v.)
  7. requirement (n.)
  8. require (v.)

Exercise C

  1. cheer
  2. Instead of
  3. encouragement
  4. popular
  5. limit
  6. course
  7. just
  8. unusual
  9. participant
  10. However

Exercise D

  1. 2. No
     2. No
     2. No
     1. Yes
     1. Yes
  2. a. men
     b. men
     c. women
     d. men

Exercise E

Answers will vary.

Exercise F

Across
  5. participant
  6. crowd
  7. at
  8. across
  9. to
  11. she
  12. runner
  13. get
  14. go
  15. course
  17. race

  18. us
  21. just
  22. fall

Down
  1. marathon
  2. limit
  3. encouragement
  4. boroughs
  6. cheer
  10. on
  15. can
  16. unusual
  17. run
  19. but
  20. all

Exercise G

  1. marathon
  2. limit
  3. oldest
  4. recently
  5. cheered
  6. participants
  7. encouragement
  8. since
  9. exciting
  10. events
  11. example
  12. race
  13. ran
  14. whole
  15. backwards

Chapter 7: Margaret Mead: The World Was Her Home

Questions after paragraphs:
  1. False
  2. b
  3. Because she was interested in people and places.
  4. Answers may vary. For example: Margaret Mead's years in college; what Margaret Mead did after college.
  5. True
  6. b
  7. nine months
  8. False
  9. a. 2
     b. 1
  10. True
  11. a
  12. young Samoan women
  13. c

14. a. 3
    b. 2
15. c

Exercise A

1. a. Because she was interested in people.
   b. Yes, because not many people studied anthropology at that time, especially women.
2. She learned their language and talked with them. She lived closely with them; she ate with them and danced with them.
3. Margaret Mead was important to anthropology because she made it a popular subject. Many people became interested in anthropology because of her work.
4. Margaret Mead was a famous American anthropologist who began her work in the 1920s. She helped make anthropology a popular subject through her books on different cultures of the world.

Exercise B

1. depend (v.)
2. dependence (n.)
3. appearance (n.)
4. appears (v.)
5. differ (v.)
6. differences (n.)
7. avoid (v.)
8. avoidance (n.)

Exercise C

1. especially
2. believe
3. remarkable
4. peaceful
5. cultures
6. As a result
7. popular
8. interested
9. until
10. details

Exercise D

Answers will vary.

Exercise E

Answers will vary.

Exercise F

Across
1. college
4. popular
7. anthropologist
12. cultures
13. interested
14. Samoa
15. details
16. speak

Down
2. especially
3. world
5. books
6. famous
8. important
9. unusual
10. remarkable
11. peaceful

Exercise G

1. graduated
2. education
3. decided
4. study
5. culture
6. about
7. learn
8. returned
9. wrote
10. book
11. popular
12. result
13. interested
14. Because
15. subject

Chapter 8: Louis Pasteur: A Modern-Day Scientist

Questions after paragraphs:
1. c
2. a deadly disease
3. a
4. a. No
   b. Because there was no cure for rabies at that time.
5. a
6. c
7. c

8. a. 1
   b. 2
9. a. 3
   b. 1
10. a
11. a. 2
    b. druggists (chemists)
    c. Today, pharmacists sell different types of medicine.
12. a. 2
    b. 1
    c. Because he worked so slowly.
13. False
14. True
15. Louis Pasteur's life as an adult (Louis Pasteur's work as an adult)
16. b
17. b
18. a
19. a. An inoculation is a shot (an injection).
    b. 3
20. Because Pasteur's vaccination cured him.
21. a
22. c
23. a
24. a. 2
    b. 3
    c. 3
25. a. 2
    b. 1

Exercise A

1. Because he enjoyed watching the town chemist help people.
2. Because Joseph was dying. If Pasteur didn't treat Joseph, he would die anyway. If Pasteur did treat Joseph, he had a chance to live.
3. a. Pasteur observed that germs cause meat and milk to spoil.
   b. He also observed that germs cause many serious diseases.
4. b

Exercise B

1. observe (v.)
2. observations (n.)
3. education (n.)
4. educated (v.)
5. vaccinations (n.)
6. vaccinate (v.)
7. continued (v.)
8. continuation (n.)

Exercise C

1. Because of
2. At first
3. decided
4. cure
5. careful
6. process
7. assisted
8. For example
9. In fact
10. curious
11. caused

Exercise D

Answers will vary.

Exercise E

Answers will vary.

Exercise F

Across
2. patient
3. deadly
4. go
5. medicine
9. not
10. spoil
12. curious
16. so
17. cure
18. sick
19. benefit
20. ate
21. vaccination
23. town
25. in

Down
1. are
2. pharmacist
3. did
4. germs
6. customers
7. all
8. inoculation
11. in
12. can
13. rabies
14. assist
15. prevent
21. very
22. too
24. we

Exercise G

1. carefully
2. learner
3. school
4. thoughtful
5. but
6. became
7. scientist
8. During
9. studied
10. illnesses
11. prevent
12. devised
13. such
14. age
15. benefit

Chapter 9: The Origin of the Moon

Questions after paragraphs:
1. a
2. False
3. False
4. a. 3
   b. 2
5. b
6. True
7. Scientists' theory about the origin of the moon.
8. b
9. a
10. b
11. a
12. b
13. a
14. b
15. b
16. c
17. False
18. a
19. b

Exercise A

1. a. 3
   b. They brought back pieces of rock.
2. Pieces of moon rock, the moon's movements, and information about the Earth and the moon
3. a. The impact theory says that a very large object hit the Earth, and many huge pieces broke off. These pieces came together and formed the moon.
   b. The moon doesn't have any water; the Earth has iron in its center, but the moon has very little iron; the Earth and the moon are almost the same age, but the moon is younger.
   c. New information may help support this theory or help show that this theory is wrong.
4. b

Exercise B

1. informed (v.)
2. information (n.)
3. formation (n.)
4. formed (v.)
5. explains (v.)
6. explanations (n.)
7. create (v.)
8. creation (n.)

Exercise C

1. guess
2. wonder
3. development
4. support
5. in the future
6. for now
7. Then
8. finally
9. but
10. Perhaps

Exercise D

Answers will vary.

Exercise E

Answers will vary.

Exercise F

Across
3. believe
5. movement
6. hot
7. yes
9. object
10. no
12. up
13. from
15. support
18. wrong
19. formed

22. put
23. theories
26. pieces
27. scientists
29. billion

Down

1. center
2. have
3. broke
4. information
5. moon
6. hit
8. explain
11. orbit
14. creates
15. she
16. prove
17. perhaps
20. impact
21. at
24. origin
25. eat
28. sun
30. is

Exercise G

1. believe
2. large
3. object
4. pieces
5. around
6. time
7. moon
8. facts
9. dry
10. heat
11. However
12. center
13. Earth
14. same
15. prove
16. future
17. either
18. wrong
19. scientists
20. theory

Chapter 10: Maps: The Keys to Our World

Questions after paragraphs:

1. Answers will vary. For example, because maps help us find places; because maps help us not get lost; because maps help us give other people accurate directions; because maps show the borders of countries and prevent wars; because maps help us learn about many places.
2. a
3. Answers will vary. For example, hundreds of years ago, maps were very inaccurate; maps had a lot of illustrations, but maps today don't; maps had blank spaces for areas where people did not have enough information.
4. Answers will vary.
5. b
6. Answers will vary. For example, historians haven't looked everywhere, and there are still old maps in China; because the maps were made of silk, they don't exist any longer.
7. Answers will vary. For example, the oldest maps represented farms and towns because these were the only areas that people knew well; because these were the only areas that people who lived there were interested in; because maps had different purposes in the past, such as showing who owned land.
8. b
9. Answers will vary. For example, how maps changed and became more accurate; how people learned that the Earth wasn't really flat.
10. a. 3
    b. 2
11. a
12. c
13. a. 3
    b. 1
14. a
15. Because people didn't travel very much.
16. c
17. a
18. c

Exercise A

1. a. 4,300-year-old clay maps in Iraq
   b. 2,000-year-old silk maps in China
   c. a 2,600-year-old clay map in Babylonia
2. They thought it was a flat circle.
3. The first map of the world looked like a flat circle. It had one ocean with several islands in it.
4. a. Eratosthenes
   b. 2,300 years ago (in the third century B.C.)
   c. He thought it was 28,600 miles (46,000 kilometers).
   d. No, it wasn't.
5. The first reliable maps of the world were made in the 1890s.
6. b

Exercise B

1. reliable (adj.)
2. reliably (adv.)
3. inexpensively (adv.)
4. inexpensive (adj.)
5. easy (adj.)
6. easily (adv.)
7. accurately (adv.)
8. accurate (adj.)

Exercise C

1. Unfortunately
2. In fact
3. Gradually
4. However
5. until
6. as long as
7. wondered
8. calculated
9. realized

Exercise D

Answers will vary.

Exercise E

Answers will vary.

Exercise F

Across
1. flat
5. areas

7. discovered
8. or
10. gradually
12. figure
13. all
16. calculate
17. sphere
20. him
21. accurate
22. did
24. maps
26. fact
27. inexpensive
31. modern
32. said

Down
2. archaeologists
3. had
4. represent
6. realize
9. reliable
11. up
12. facts
14. as
15. measurement
18. draw
19. can
23. depend
24. me
25. planets
28. put
29. very
30. not

Exercise G

1. maps
2. countries
3. even
4. planets
5. useful
6. invention
7. centuries
8. first
9. Ancient
10. ideas
11. draw
12. until
13. around
14. time
15. began
16. accurate
17. not
18. inexpensive
19. depend
20. without

Chapter 11: Saving Lives with Weather Forecasting

Questions after paragraphs:
1. b
2. True
3. a
4. b
5. Next Generation Weather Radar; it is a weather-service radar.
6. a
7. True
8. c
9. a
10. c
11. 152
12. b
13. False
14. True
15. a
16. c
17. b

Exercise A

1. Because usually many people die when a massive tornado strikes.
2. It helped weather forecasters warn people that the tornado was coming.
3. They relied on eyewitness reports.
4. Yes, because fewer people will die if they are warned ahead of time.
5. b

Exercise B

1. avoided (v.)
2. Avoidance (n.)
3. occurrence (n.)
4. occur (v.)
5. dependence (n.)
6. depends (v.)
7. resist (v.)
8. resistance (n.)

Exercise C

1. obsolete
2. indispensable
3. severe
4. Consequently
5. accurately
6. Amazingly
7. decreases
8. predicts
9. warned
10. destroyed

Exercise D

1. 2, 4, 1, 3
Other answers will vary.

Exercise E

Answers will vary.

Exercise F

Across
1. system
4. are
6. weather
8. did
11. decreased
13. indispensable
16. destructive
18. forecasters
19. all
21. yes
22. predict
23. eat
24. sure

Down
1. state
2. sphere
3. me
5. radar
6. warning
7. had
9. ordinarily
10. can
12. amazingly
14. end
15. accurate
17. tornadoes
18. flat
20. occur
22. put

Exercise G

1. characteristic
2. obsolete
3. eyewitness
4. prepare
5. late
6. severe
7. warning
8. predict
9. percentage
10. lower
11. occur
12. all

13. only
14. tornado
15. several
16. hour
17. destructive
18. accurately
19. indispensable
20. weather

Chapter 12: Clues and Criminal Investigation

Questions after paragraphs:
1. b
2. c
3. c
4. Answers will vary. For example, the types of clues that investigators/experts look for; how experts look for and find clues.
5. b
6. a. 1
   b. footprints, fingerprints, lip prints on glasses, hair, blood, clothing fibers, bullet shells
7. b
8. Answers will vary. For example, how clues are analyzed in a laboratory; what experts find out by analyzing clues.
9. b
10. a
11. a. 2
    b. 1
12. a. 1
    b. 2
13. b
14. a. 2
    b. 1
15. c
16. c
17. a. 1
    b. 2
    c. 1

Exercise A

1. All crime experts believe that a criminal always brings something to the scene of a crime and always leaves something there.
2. Because the person who committed a crime may have his or her fingerprints on file from a crime he or she committed before.
3. Perhaps the victim and the murderer had a fight or struggle, and the murderer was hurt.
4. Because these clues help to identify the specific person who was at the scene of the crime, and who may have committed the crime.
5. c

Exercise B

1. skillful (adj.)
2. skill (n.)
3. successful (adj.)
4. success (n.)
5. help (n.)
6. helpful (adj.)
7. careful (adj.)
8. care (n.)

Exercise C

1. suspect
2. expert
3. principle
4. evidence
5. if
6. Consequently
7. Furthermore
8. investigated
9. occurred
10. suspected

Exercise D

Answers will vary.

Exercise E

Answers will vary.

Exercise F

Across
1. bullet
6. distinctive
11. principle
13. experts
15. are
16. victim
18. all
21. rare
22. got
23. analyze
24. innocent
27. suspect

Down

2. unique
3. too
4. as
5. DNA
7. ill
8. up
9. fingerprints
10. occur
12. at
13. evidence
14. solve
17. instance
19. say
20. crimes
22. guilty
25. can
26. let

Exercise G

1. crime
2. start
3. evidence
4. belief
5. leaves
6. result
7. careful
8. occurred
9. case
10. Furthermore
11. uses
12. gun
13. scene
14. Experts
15. bullet
16. specific
17. Consequently
18. suspect
19. clues
20. guilty